INSTINCTIVE
PARENTING

INSTINCTIVE PARENTING

Trusting Ourselves to Raise Good Kids

ADA CALHOUN

GALLERY BOOKS
New York   London   Toronto   Sydney

Gallery Books
A Division of Simon & Schuster, Inc.
1230 Avenue of the Americas
New York, NY 10020

First Gallery Books hardcover edition March 2010

GALLERY BOOKS and colophon are trademarks of Simon & Schuster, Inc.

For information about special discounts for bulk purchases,
please contact Simon & Schuster Special Sales at 1-866-506-1949
or business@simonandschuster.com.

The Simon & Schuster Speakers Bureau can bring authors to your live event. For more information or to book an event contact the Simon & Schuster Speakers Bureau at 1-866-248-3049 or visit our website at www.simonspeakers.com.

Designed by Jaime Putorti

Manufactured in the United States of America

10   9   8   7   6   5   4   3   2   1

Library of Congress Cataloging-in-Publication Data
Calhoun, Ada.
    Instinctive parenting : trusting ourselves to raise good kids / by Ada Calhoun.
        p. cm.
    1. Child rearing. I. Title.
    HQ769.C284 2010
    649'.1—dc22
2009032605

ISBN 978-1-4391-5729-9
ISBN 978-1-4391-6573-7 (ebook)

For Neal

Contents

PART TWO: Food

PART THREE: Love

How I Learned to Stop Worrying and Love the Baby

It was a beautiful day at the park. My two-year-old son was running around a tree with one of his best friends. I was chatting with his friend's mother. The sun was shining. The kids were giddy. I was comfortable—too comfortable.

The boy's mother asked about Babble.com, the online parenting magazine I helped found. She said she checked it every day and loved all the controversies it covers.

"It's ironic that I edit a controversial site," I said cheerily, "because I'm the most traditional parent ever. Oliver is Ferberized, circumcised, baptized, and vaccinated. Not a hip decision in the bunch."

The mother said nothing, but I saw her go pale. She backed slowly away in horror.

I realized what an idiot I'd been to rattle off those things, each a bullet in a gun with which parents on the playground enjoy shooting each other. Her son was probably none of those things. She was a yoga teacher, for goodness sake. What was I thinking?

"Baptized?" she finally asked, stricken.

The thing is, our kids love each other. I really like her. But these days, parenting decisions carry an absurd weight. Whether you let your kid watch TV, how long you let your child use a pacifier, whether you weaned your nursing baby at three months or nine months or nine years—all of it identifies you as one kind of parent or another, and those seemingly insignificant decisions can prove more divisive than national politics.

And it's not just a trend among a certain class of wealthy women with too much time on their hands. No, these days it's everyone: poor and rich; urban, rural, and suburban; age twenty or forty-five. We all want to do the best by our children, but now no one is entirely sure what "the best" is. Go online and Google *circumcision* or *vaccination* or *sleep-training* and see if you can find a consensus, a middle ground.

What you *do* find is opposing, entrenched camps, their tents pitched and their flags flying: the people who swear letting your child "cry it out" will scar him for life, the people who insist that not circumcising will automatically lead to STDs in your future daughter-in-law, the people who identify absolutely every item in your household as a trigger for autism.

Even in polite conversation, you are apt to discover that something innocuous you have done (opting not to use a baby monitor, choosing to go back to work when your baby was young, breastfeeding a toddler) is a form of child abuse by someone else's standards. Often you will not be called a terrible parent on the spot. But you may well be told, "Oh, you're so *brave*." Or, "You're so much more *relaxed* about parenting than I am." Or, my favorite, "Wow! *I* could never do *that*!"

Even in their mock humility, these parents are certain of their rightness. And when faced with alternative viewpoints,

ADA CALHOUN

many of these advocates for their parenting positions become surprisingly furious. Check out those overly intense comment threads on parenting message boards and note the burning eyes of people who argue about the pros or cons of pre-kindergarten.

What does it have to do with them how you raise your child, assuming you're not doing anything cruel and unusual? Why can't each parent just work it out for his or her own family? Why must they be so angry with people who do something else? Who is being served by this cult of perfection?

I suspect that it has to do with a collective loss of faith in our instinctive ability to raise our children in a way that keeps us, and our children, happy and fulfilled. Of course we can flip through some books. We can solicit help from our pediatrician, who has seen many more babies than we have. We can ask (without our own agenda!) friends and parents and strangers what they did. Through trial and error, we can land on workable solutions for our own unique situations. Keeping a kid alive and reasonably well behaved and well adjusted until he's eighteen isn't rocket science, and our attempts to accomplish that simple goal shouldn't be torture. Yes, parenting is hard, but it doesn't have to be so *complicated*.

And yet we've betrayed ourselves time and again by assuming we don't know anything, and by trusting in supposedly higher powers, like the latest expert making their rounds on the morning shows, the loudest mother at the barbecue, or the most aggressive poster to a blog. There seems to be an evangelical cult around every little decision—about, say, when to start solid food—each with followers looking to convert you. The late-start camp will raise its eyebrows at anyone who breaks out the smooshed bananas at four months.

But there is hope for us. We can abandon the anxiety, the judgment, and the insecurity. We can do what works for us and see those choices as a few possible routes among many that all end in the same place: our kids growing up into their own identities. Depending on how we raise them, the kids may be a little more or less prepared for certain things, more or less neurotic, but regardless of whether we go with the Maclaren or the Chicco, our children will be the same people they were going to be anyway.

Plenty of things keep me up at night. There are days I feel completely overwhelmed. Being a parent sometimes still seems impossibly difficult. (Like, how do you not throttle a big kid on the playground who's mean to your toddler? This I'm working on.) But I have gotten to the point where I don't want to read any divisive books, watch any fear-mongering segments on TV, listen to any self-proclaimed experts telling me what I should be doing. I just don't want to hear it.

And I've realized that pretty much every time I've passed judgment on a fellow parent, I've later come to find myself in their same shoes and not doing all that much better with the challenge. Of course it can be fun to talk smack on others. I'd be lying if I said I didn't enjoy the occasional gossip session with one parent about another. And yet, the truth is that, ultimately, there is almost no supposedly off-beat decision that I haven't seen work out just fine for someone.

That's why I basically hate advice-driven parenting books, magazines, and blogs. Some are certainly worse than others, but almost all of them have a tone that's either too cutesy or too condescending. When I was made editor in chief of Babble, a brand-new parenting site at the end of 2006, I was a few months pregnant. I'd been a babysitter all through high school and college, and doted on a few nieces and nephews and friends' kids, and one particularly delightful goddaughter, but that was the extent of my parenting expertise.

When I was hugely pregnant with my son, Oliver, and then when I was nursing a newborn, I enjoyed flipping through books for week-by-week pictures of babies in utero or for little bits of applicable wisdom. "My baby is the size of a lime!" I would remark, looking in wonder from my belly to the book. "He is getting foremilk, and then hindmilk!" I would observe, as I looked approvingly from the book to my nursing new-born.

And yet, I began to notice that none of this information ever really *helped*. Some of it was cool, sure, and fun to read, but none of it made my life easier. In fact, it often confused me or made me doubt my instincts. When my son threw his arms out to his sides just as he was falling asleep, I could smugly tell my husband, Neal, "That's the Moro reflex. He feels like he's falling. That's why babies usually prefer sleeping on their stomachs, because then they don't get that."

"So let's put him on his stomach," Neal suggested, reasonably.

"No! We're not allowed. Babies have to sleep on their backs. We could swaddle him to prevent him from flailing."

"But he hates being swaddled."

"True."

So really it turned out to be useless reading those books. Plus, one night it almost wound up getting us divorced.

In those first weeks, my husband sweetly got up each night for the three a.m. feeding and gave the baby a bottle. One night, I woke up a little and heard him go to the fridge and warm up a bottle and feed it to our son. Then I heard him lay our son in his cradle by our bed.

I couldn't help it; I had to look at Oliver's sweet, sated, sleeping face, so I rolled over and looked into the cradle. There he was, eyes open and sucking away at a bottle *propped up in front of him on a blanket.*

I completely freaked out. I started yelling at my husband about "pair bonds" and "associating food with comfort." I snatched Oliver up into my arms and held him extra tight to make up for the minutes of contact-free eating.

See, I had just read a chapter in one of the more aggressive attachment parenting books about how if babies are not cuddled while being fed they grow up to be sociopaths—at least that was how I'd remembered it. Probably I was exaggerating exactly how horrible the author thought the propped bottle was, but I don't think by much. He definitely thought it was a huge mistake.

My husband was, rightly, furious at my accusation that he had done something bad when in fact he was doing something lovely—giving the baby nourishment in the middle of the night so I could get a break from breastfeeding every few hours and get a decent chunk of sleep. Palpably angry, he took the baby from me, continued feeding him, and said, "I had to go to the bathroom. I was away from the baby for five minutes tops. You need to throw those books away."

He was right. The passage about the dreaded propped bottle had made me into a fanatic opponent of something that was, upon further reflection, a very practical solution to a very normal problem: needing to accomplish two things at once.

What should Neal have done instead? Woken me up? Not gone to the bathroom no matter how desperate he became?

ADA CALHOUN

Tried to pee while balancing a weeks-old baby and a bottle in his arms? He picked the most logical option. I got to keep sleeping (or I would have if I hadn't been so crazy). The baby got to eat. Neal got to relieve himself. We had a happy baby, a happy household. It wasn't "perfect," but it was good. And that made me think there was something wrong with the experts' notion of perfection. Thank you, night of the evil propped bottle, for you showed me the light!

Luckily, running a parenting site gave me a sense of authority I could internalize. From my perch, I could see just how many different childcare setups there were out there, and how many different parenting styles existed, and how many different techniques for discipline, sleep, and feeding. And I could see that most of them, when it came down to it, worked out fine, *as long as they emerged more or less organically from the family.* If the story of the technique was a book, that usually spelled doom. If the strategy emerged from a family's attempts to find their own particular way of accomplishing something, the result was usually great.

For that reason, I don't think the same advice is right for any two families. I have friends I would like to tell to lighten up and I have friends I think could stand to be a little stricter. But they're all totally fine parents and it's totally their business what kind of parents they want to be. What I think is more important than having yet another bunch of data and opinions is having a basic framework to filter all the bits of news and products and health studies hailing down on us. What I'm proposing instead of still more information is a filter through which to look at all these sources.

This book is a call for postpartisan parenting, free of self-righteousness or slavish devotion to any one parenting guru.

I'm convinced that the key is focusing on the very few things that matter (making sure you are raising a kind person and making that person feel loved) and then doing whatever the hell you want about the rest (bedtime, schooling, feeding, social life, friends, housing—everything else, really). Parenting is so much simpler and so much more fun than squabbles over the "right" way to wean, to dress your child, to hold him, make it seem. There is, after all, purity only in death.

When a friend of mine said, shamefacedly, that she'd quit breastfeeding after a few months because she'd had so many problems with it and really had to work and sleep, I told her she was right, that she'd already given her baby all the miraculous immune stuff breastfeeding promises, so she should feel exceedingly proud of herself. I said she had knocked herself out to do right by her baby, and that she also knew her limits.

And the fact was, four months or whatever she'd managed, was great. It was far more important, I said, to do an honest cost-benefit analysis. And in this case, it sounded as if it was overall better for her family if she weaned her baby. In doing so, she was not failing to live up to an objective notion of perfection. What she was doing was perfect—for *her* child, who in this case needed her mother's sanity and income more than she needed breast milk.

I added that her child was one of the happiest, sweetest, healthiest children on earth and so why should she give a second's thought to some arbitrary standard she's supposed to meet? Yes, the World Health Organization recommends two years of nursing. Yes, La Leche League says you should let children self-wean (and that even if the child wants to wean, you shouldn't go down without a fight!). But this was *her* baby and *her* middle-of-the-night feedings, and *her* job offers. What works as international policy doesn't work for every single person on the planet, with every single child.

My confidence in these matters is based on two things:

One: in my observation, it matters hardly at all which parenting philosophy parents adopt or what they do; the kids do what they're genetically predisposed to do, more or less. Character is pretty set from the start; it's just a question of bringing out the better stuff and mediating the worse.

Two: the parents who spend the most time agonizing over their decisions often have the most messed-up kids.

For real: on the playground, the boys with the fashionably long hair and the organic-cotton T-shirts and the ergonomic wooden pedal-free bikes from Sweden and the locally grown chickpeas for snacks are inevitably snatching toys out of the supposedly ill-raised kids' hands.

And I think that's because among the hyperparenting crowd there's been a collective missing of the point. The point is not high-tech strollers, "mommy wars," or preschool admissions. The point is not the organic content of your snacks, the breathability of your baby clothes, or the number of Caldecott Award winners in your child's library. The point is bringing up a person to be in the world, around other people.

The parents with the checklists and the cross-referenced parenting guidebooks and the twenty subscriptions to daily newsletters with development trackers and the fetishistic attention to charts and the binders full of information on schools within a twenty-mile radius are not happier than the parents who just kind of amble through the whole thing with the baggies of salty pretzels and the shoddy plastic toys from the drugstore. Nor are they necessarily less happy. No way is the one true path.

Regardless of how hyper or mellow we choose to be, we owe it to ourselves to trust our instincts and tune out the noise around parenting choices. We also owe it to one another to stop obsessing over what other people are doing. It's so much less complicated and stressful than we're making it. There are only three things we have to give our kids: shelter, food, and love, so I will donate a section to the variables of each.

Shelter can be a house, apartment, shack, or a tent in the desert that moves each day. Inhabiting that home can be one or two parents, or someone else entirely. These caretakers can work or stay home or some combination. There can be a lot of sleep or a little under this roof, and there can be many toys or none.

Food can be lavishly home-cooked meals, takeout, or a few years' worth of French fries. Breastfeeding can be involved, or not. During pregnancy, the mother could have eaten an impeccable medley of vegetables and grains at every meal, or grilled cheese three times a day.

Love just means showing your child he's loved. You can recognize a well-loved child when you see her. She has a faint glow of security about her, a sense that whatever else may be true, the world is basically an okay place. And secure children are usually the most able to then direct love to other people.

That's really it: shelter, food, and love. The second we have a baby, our instinct is to provide those things to the best of our ability. The details are unimportant.

Of course you may well say, if parenting is instinctive and that's all there is to it and I hate parenting advice books, why is this book necessary? Well, I think we're at a crisis point. Too many parents are making themselves and their kids stressed out for no reason. For my friends who want to have kids but are scared, or who are pregnant and are terrified, I wanted to communicate these things: that they can have children without losing their own identity, or their partners, or their enjoyment of the world. This is the book I wish I had gotten at my baby shower (not that the cookbooks weren't *lovely*).

This book isn't intended as a substitution for all other parenting books, nor is it some slacker book that says you never have to care about anything. It's also not just one more opinion about whether or not you should circumcise, sleep-train, or use a pacifier. That stuff is *so* none of my business. But I think, or at least I hope, it will provide a reality check to all that other stuff, a balance and a soothing counterargument to all the hyped You Musts. That's what usually makes me feel better when I hit a wall with parenting—honest, illustrative stories from other parents in the trenches about what they did in the same situation. I think that's kind of a universal desire when you have small kids: reassurance that whatever it is you're facing, you're not alone.

When it comes to all the health topics, everyone already knows all the pros and cons. People don't need more information. There is so much data out there, you absorb it by osmosis. Whether you've read a stack of parenting tomes or only flipped through magazines a few times or peeked at a couple of message boards, you probably have more information about any given topic than you could ever use.

I am the mother of a toddler, the stepmother of a teenager. They are fantastic kids, I love them to bits, and as of press time they seem to be okay with me. But I have nowhere near what you would call expertise. I'm new to this mothering thing. Any old parent who passes me on the street has just as much wisdom about childcare.

Which is sort of the point of this book. We all know about the same amount. We're all working it out. If all these people who insist they know a lot more than we do would just get out of our heads, we could do this thing with a lot less anxiety and a lot more friends.

My son's friend's yoga teacher mother has been able to overlook all the apparently crazy conservative things I've done with my kid, because we are still friendly. I even watched her son while she recovered from delivering his sister in an unmedicated home birth in her apartment. Her kid and mine ate hot dogs, drank chocolate milk, and watched *The Backyardigans*. We all had a wonderful time.

PART ONE

Shelter

On Shelter

Today's new parents did not grow up in the most secure homes. Our parents divorced in record numbers—close to one in three—and made independence a priority over security.[1] They were, many of them quite proudly, hands off. Rejecting *their* parents' paternalism, they decided they were going to level with us, to be straightforward and honest and raise us to be freethinkers. Many of us were latchkey kids, watched ridiculous amounts of television, and became our parents' confidants, their "friends."

Watch some '70s TV and see if you can find a euphemism or a "don't worry about it."[2] Nope. What you *can* find: poverty, racism, and natural disasters. Our parents weren't, as a generation, particularly parental. We weren't coddled, to say the least. Many of our homes were broken, in one way or another.

So as a new generation of parents, we're overcompensating. We are, proudly, hands on. We're carrying our babies around in slings until they can walk, researching the hell out of our school districts, and asking our pediatricians five thousand questions at our routine well-baby visits. We're trying to provide the best, most nurturing environment possible, and in the process many of us are driving ourselves crazy.

We are ambitious, trying to be the very best parents we can be, even if it means a certain level of martyrdom. The result:

we are nurturing to a fault. I can't tell you how many weird sleep arrangements I've heard about. The only way one family I know can get any sleep is if the mother and the child sleep in the bed and the husband sleeps on an air mattress on the floor.

We're in a tough spot, really, when it comes to creating a nest for our family. We're trying to do a better job than our parents, but since we've eschewed their help, we're cobbling together a parenting strategy from the Internet, our friends, and whatever memories we have of happiness as children (thus, the recent *Sesame Street: Old School* DVD release and Playskool's revamped Sit 'n Spin). We have an overload of information—plenty of it ridiculous, much of it contradictory, very little of it ringing completely true to us.

As if that weren't enough pressure, we're also really, really busy. How many couples do you know who can easily afford to have one parent stay home full-time, or to have both partners go part-time? Gen X employees work 45.6 hours a week on average, and more women are in the workforce than ever.[3] It's even more challenging to create a warm and nurturing environment when it's a struggle just to find time to vacuum.

Even those of us lucky enough to work a couple of days a week at home, or to telecommute, are tied to our e-mail or BlackBerries even when we're away from the office. (In May 2009, CNN.com called this weisure, as in work plus leisure.[4] The name actually is appropriate, because it is an ugly word and the intrusion of work into every second of our home lives is kind of gross, too.)

Couples are piecing together a living wage from multiple jobs per family, some full-time, some part-time, some work-at-home, so both parents have hectic schedules to manage. Add to that the kids' schedules, and you have a cluttered calendar leaving far too little room for relaxing and enjoying one another, but plenty of room for regret and frustration and a sense that life is living you rather than the other way around.

The Baby Boomers were laissez-faire about a lot of things when it came to child-rearing. Mostly through ignorance but also by proclivity, they weren't too concerned with protecting their kids from cigarette smoke or lead paint, let alone the unvarnished ugliness about the world. Many are the '70s children who skipped directly from learning about Columbus and his ships to a lesson in oppression and hegemony. Think the women of our parents' generation did the equivalent of a hundred Google searches trying to figure out if it was okay to have a glass of wine in the third trimester? Please. The cork was out of that bottle before you could say *Electric Company*.

And yet, in our rebellion against our parents, we've arguably gone too far in the other direction. The shelter we're providing our kids is a little too . . . sheltering. If we raise our kids too much in reaction to others—our parents, the so-called experts, the other parents on the playground, the medical establishment—we're guaranteed to make just as many mistakes, only different ones. But if we encourage our kids to be kind and generous and we trust our own instincts about all the other stuff, we may just be able to create a happy household for our family.

A Design Opportunity

In a recent article about nursery decorating, an interior designer insisted that babies' rooms must be clutter-free, painted in muted colors, and carpeted.[5]

Or what?

My son sleeps in a cluttered, red room that is also an office. I refuse to believe this has any effect on his health, well-being, or future. When the lights are out, the Plaza Hotel and an alley look the same.

It's not that pretty things aren't nice to have. It's not like I wouldn't take an extra room in our 500-square-foot apartment. (When an acquaintance recently told me her house had 14,000 square feet, I was so shocked I knocked over my drink.) I'm certainly not anticonsumerist. One of my favorite parts of traveling is hitting gift shops—sometimes before the important historical and cultural sites to which they are attached.

But the boom of pricey and stylish nursery gear has given rise to a belief that high-end baby furnishings—the "sleek, modern" nursery aesthetic, the high-tech gear, and the booming childproofing business—are necessary rather than fully optional. It's amazing how we can come to believe we must maintain a certain standard of living at all costs.

One of my favorite examples: in December 2007, a family on the Upper West Side of New York placed an ad in *New York* magazine pleading for $1 million to buy an apartment so they could stay in their wealthy neighborhood.[6]

It read:

> WE NEED HELP BUYING AN APARTMENT on the UWS, 3bd 2 bath. YOU are a philanthropic, wealthy person who would not miss a million bucks and would be interested in donating (or even investing) in a highly targeted manner: to my family. WE are a wonderful, hard working middle class family who contributes to our UWS community, is entrenched, happy and desperately wants to remain on the UWS (lest the city lose yet another wonderful family to the burbs). We can afford 600-700K, so you see the predicament. Can you help us?

No word on whether or not the ad brought them a windfall, but I hope not. Living within your means wasn't in vogue in 2007, but since the market crash, making do is definitely in.

I love our apartment for many reasons, but one of the biggest reasons is that we can afford the rent even in tough months. Sure, we need a lot of shelving to make up for the lack of space, but thank God for Ikea.

Buying an apartment or house has never been an option for us, but many of our friends pour tons of time and energy and money into their housing. Some of them can afford it and make the reasonable calculation that for them having more space or a yard, or living in a better school district, is worth sacrificing other things.

For others, home décor has become something of a fetish and having children has just added another design opportunity. In the process, they've bought themselves into a hole. It's no surprise that never in history has a generation spent so much and saved so little.

So what's the reasoning behind our amped-up nesting drive?

Generation X expert Susan Gregory Thomas argues that because of our own rather lonely childhoods, we're knocking ourselves out as parents to try to provide a homey home for our children, and that we're therefore agonizing over the littlest details of our dwellings. She writes

> We may still see ourselves as outsiders, snickering cynics who see through baby boomers' pretenses. But that's a big cover-up to hide that we're big mush-balls underneath. We are completely, utterly attached to our children. Generation Xers, the parents of the majority of young children now, are by all accounts the most devoted to family in American history. And we'll do whatever we have to do to keep them from having the crappy childhood that we had.[7]

At a party, I was telling an acquaintance about Thomas's article and I saw her bristle. "Everyone nests!" she said, somewhat defensively. "A parent buying a thousand-dollar Netto crib is no different than any young married couple painting their house and getting a blender!"

It may be that Gen Xers are only nesting, same as ever. But it's hard to deny they're doing it on a much more accelerated level than any generation in American history. Gen Xers are more involved than other consumers, and like to be a part of every decision, big and small.[8] In other words, the Boomers may have said, "I want some shag carpeting over there"; Gen X parents specify grout grade.

Our overachieving on the home front matches our over-achieving on the parenting front. And in both cases, even when we don't go all out, we feel that we should have. "The house is a mess," is not just a faux-modest throwaway line; it's a philosophy of *never enough* that we're wedded to.

The truth is: We should avoid flaking lead paint. We should avoid neighborhoods so dangerous that we're physically afraid in them. We should aim for a place with heating and/or cooling as necessary to keep everyone from getting frostbite or heatstroke. Beyond that, who cares? Kids certainly don't care. Especially when they're little, they just want to be around their parents and/or other people who love them. For the first few years, they have very low expectations. They can't tell a Tiffany teether from a Target spoon, or a palatial six-bedroom house from a tiny two-room apartment. As long as it's got a loving family in it, it's just home.

Who Are the People
in Your Neighborhood?

The push to be in a "good" neighborhood can create a false need to live beyond our means. And what makes for a good neighborhood is very hard to determine. Good for whom? Kids don't care about property values or hipness. And there's very little advantage to living around rich people, especially if you can't afford to.

In plenty of ways, poorer neighborhoods are actually way better than rich ones for children. Everything—groceries, laundry, and haircuts—is cheaper. Families crammed together in apartment buildings or close-knit communities tend to lean on one another more than those walled away in McMansions. Kids' educational success has a lot to do with their parents' reading to them and exposing them to culture. If you live in a cheaper place than you can afford, you can use the $500 a month you're saving on rent to buy books and go to museums.

We live in a New York City neighborhood that reminds me of the old *Sesame Street*. Everyone knows one another. People still sit out on their stoops. Spanish and English are spoken interchangeably. I swear, Oliver thought his name was *Que lindo!* ("How beautiful!") for the first year of his life, so often did he hear it as we strolled him around the neighborhood.

It's amazing, too, how much having a baby made us feel a sense of community. We were all but invisible before we had a child. My husband and I walked around, passing people on the street, and we hardly noticed that we saw the same people every day. But as soon as we had a baby, we showed up on our neighbors' radar and we got to know them.

Upstairs, there are the teenage kids who make Oliver laugh and whose father is a Mets fan like us. Down the block, the grandmother who sits out on a swing with her Chihuahua named Brownie gives Oliver toy cars and asks him about his day on the playground. He taught himself to swing on her gate, climbing aboard and lifting the latch so he flies by laughing.

Behind the deli counter on the corner is Shorty, who seems to work twenty-four hours a day but who always has time to shout, "Hey, Big Boy!" from behind the turkey slicer, and to ask Oliver what trucks he's seen lately. The local repairman high-fives Oliver on our way to nursery school. Some mornings, it takes us a full ten minutes to get down the block because we have to stop and say hello so often.

I didn't think I would like being part of a neighborhood. I used to like anonymity. But it turns out that having everyone note your comings and goings is kind of fantastic. I hope Oliver will never wander out our front door alone, but if he does, I know that a dozen people would intercept him on his way to score M&Ms from Shorty.

I like that we're a part of something larger than ourselves. Oliver feels appreciated by people he passes on the street. If I'm away from the house all day, I return to reports from multiple sources. "Your mother was in here with Oliver this afternoon," the deli guy will tell me; "they got Dots." Down the block: "Your husband took Oliver to the park this morning and they were singing 'Twinkle Twinkle Little Star,'" Gloria will say. "He's getting so big!" "Oliver was with a new babysitter today, huh?" Zaida will report from her swing. "They walked right by us. It's okay, she didn't know who we are!"

This is one reason I like raising a child in the city. That, and it's so easy to find ways to entertain a kid. Oliver loves the subway, loves museums, and loves parks. We can go to the American Museum of Natural History and spend hours looking at the ocean life dioramas. We can go to the Met and spend hours with the totem poles. There are dozens of different kinds of food around, so Oliver has a broad palate and knows he likes *paratha* bread, lo mein, and dumplings of all kinds.

And yet, I get why people often leave the city when they have kids. Sometimes dragging around a kid on the subways is exhausting. For the same rent we pay on our tiny apartment, we could have a house with a yard somewhere else. The work world in the city is very competitive, so it's not like you can ever just coast.

And it's amazing to see Oliver in the country, how much he loves running through fields, trying to catch frogs, stomping in a stream. I'm sure he would be just as happy living in the woods.

And the suburbs? When he gets to play with a bunch of kids, just running back and forth on grass or pavement for a few hours, he's in heaven. So that would work fine, too. And we'd have enough square footage so he could actually maneuver his trike inside without running over shoes, the cat, and the mail.

I'm glad that I grew up in the city, but when I was about ten I visited my cousins in the suburbs and came back furious with my parents. In Ohio, I had hung out on lawns in kiddie pools; I had gone to a drive-through for root beer floats; I had played in yards until dusk. "You never told me it could be like that!" I yelled at my poor urban parents when I returned.

Everywhere is a potentially good place to raise a kid. I'm often surprised when people move out of cities when they have kids so "they can have a childhood." People who move when they have kids should be honest: wanting more space or green grass or clean air is of course totally reasonable. But it's not really for the kids; it's for the parents, who don't want to worry about speeding taxis. Kids can be happy (or miserable, for that matter) anywhere on earth.

How Much Negativity Is Helpful?

When I announced I was pregnant at a family dinner, I expected delight, enthusiasm, and joy. And there was that for a few minutes. "We're so happy for you!" one person gushed. "You're going to be great parents!"

We beamed.

But then there were two more hours of something else.

"After the first three months it's great, but those first three months are pure hell on earth," said one person at the dinner.

His wife nodded. "Hell," she confirmed.

"It's not so much gaining a child as losing a wife," my father quipped to Neal.

There was more: talk of no sleep, of no money, of strained relationships.

As this went on, I got more and more weepy. I brushed away a tear here and there with my cloth napkin.

Finally, I burst into sobs. "I just want to hear good things!" I wailed. "When I sat down at the table I was so *haaaappy!*"

Everyone looked at me like I was crazy. They didn't think they were being unreasonably negative. They thought they were being honest and realistic and not sugarcoating everything. They thought they were doing me a *favor*.

But I was only a month pregnant. I had eight months to be prepared for the realities of new parenthood. I thought I had a little more time just to revel. It made me wish I'd waited until the recommended twelve weeks to tell everyone I was pregnant. It would have been my own special, naively happy little secret.

"Of course it's wonderful to have a baby!" everyone said. "I just wasn't prepared for the hard parts," one woman said, "so I always try to make sure I tell people it's not all rainbows and glitter. That it's tough, sometimes grueling . . ."

"You're doing it again," I said.

"Sorry," she said. "It's a hard habit to break. But obviously it's the best thing in the world to have a baby. You're going to have a great baby."

I could see her biting her tongue to keep the "but . . ." from escaping, and I was glad she did. I just wanted to enjoy the new life growing inside me and to imagine our future. I knew it wouldn't all be easy. I didn't care, and I didn't want to think about that yet. All the doom talk was killing my elated hormonal buzz, and I sensed that they didn't totally know what they were talking about. Our situation was different than that of the other couples at the table: My job had some flexibility. My husband was home. We had moved into a cheap apartment and were on our way out of credit card debt. We had a lot of friends.

Cut to two years later.

Okay, yes, there were hardships. Some of what they said was dead-on. Some of the things they warned me about were no-joke tough.

Nursing while working full-time was hard. Going in just two days a week sounded great, but being away from Oliver for ten hours in a row those two days a week really felt lousy.

At times I did resent my husband for not being a Rocke-feller so that I could have quit my job if I wanted. (The fact that even if I could have, I would not have quit didn't seem to matter to my addled brain.) My husband was doing the major-ity of the baby care and couldn't do any of his own work, espe-cially when I started doing three days a week in the office. He wound up spending a whole year with our son almost twenty-four hours a day. I was with him all but two or three days a week. And yet, it felt like there was always so much to do. There were many days that somehow went by both grindingly slowly and too fast to find time to wash the dishes.

There were days I was brutally tired, frustrated, and spent. But I never despaired, because I was so in love with my baby, and I think it was a lot easier because he was an unusually happy kid. Friends whose babies had colic or who were extra-demanding didn't fare so well.

But I also never despaired *out of spite*. So many people had told me how impossible it was, that I was determined to prove them wrong. I found myself talking in platitudes when I met a pregnant woman. "It's the best thing *ever*," I heard myself saying. "People will tell you it is definitely going to be super-hard at first, but don't you believe them! It doesn't *have* to be anything!"

It's cyclical like this, I think: you counterbalance the advice you got.

In August 2007, a commenter on the blog Strollerderby wrote, "All I hear from my generation is the negative, how it will ruin your relationship, your body, your sense of self. Now that I finally had the guts to get pregnant, I'm just trying not to be so anxious about how bad everyone assures me it will be."[9]

My friend Gwynne Watkins agreed in a post called "I'm Pregnant—Tell Me Something Good!"[10] She wrote

I've been dismayed by the number of people who've responded to the news by cackling maniacally and telling me I have no idea what I'm in for, or that I'll never sleep again . . . I grew up reading cynical postfeminist news stories about how women actually can't have it all. And for every story I hear about how raising children is the best thing I'll ever do, I've heard ten about how it will forever ruin my career, body, and sex life. Frankly, I could use a few more people telling me that being a mom is an awesome thing.

On the other side of the spectrum are books like Susan Maushart's *The Mask of Motherhood: How Becoming a Mother Changes Our Lives and Why We Never Talk About It*. Maushart argues that we have an obligation to talk about how hard motherhood can be. "It is no exaggeration," she writes, "to say that we owe it not only to our own mental health but to the very future of the species to take motherhood seriously, to strip off the masks we have been wearing, and to see with clear eyes and speak with open voices about the realities we experience."[11]

That was a decade ago, and if it was true back then that the dark side is hidden, that sure isn't the case now. The Internet has made it possible for mothers, and fathers, to unload about all the "realities," from postpartum depression to diaper contents. Private life and private thoughts need never stay private. All the masks Maushart speaks of have come clattering down. And in many ways this is a wonderful thing: at three in the morning, you can find someone just as pregnant as you with tips on morning sickness. You can find another parent who is ambivalent about her parenting skills, or who has an extra Pack 'n Play to sell.

What *is* a problem is getting beyond the complaining and commiseration. The world needs to change, to become easier on new parents—to make access to food and education possible for everyone, and to make it easier for workers in the United States to spend more than a few anxious weeks at home with their newborns before they have to head back to work—and to then somehow make everything work despite limited access to affordable daycare. So let's all start talking about changing the situation rather than about how to raise or lower the expectations of a vulnerable parent-to-be.

Registering: What You *Really* Need in the Nursery

We were at Coney Island last summer with our ratty light-weight stroller, and I noticed that no one on the boardwalk or on the beach had one of those high-end vehicles with the great shocks, tailor-made for bumpy boardwalk rides and off-roading. In fact, I realized that the only time I ever saw those thousand-dollar strollers was when they were being pushed around uptown by nannies. Smooth sidewalks. No need for any advanced swivel features.

So who are those superexpensive things for? The list of registry "must-haves" gets longer by the year, and the status symbols get more ludicrous. Those thousand-dollar strollers are common, as are $40 3M T-shirts.

Pick up a parenting magazine or check a parenting blog and you are hit with a particular set of cultural pressures about where you're *supposed* to live, how you're *supposed* to behave, what you're *supposed* to own. But who has set these standards? The most liberating thing in the world can be the realization that there are almost no "necessities."

There's nothing wrong with some cute baby bunting, a nightlight, or an industrial breast pump. But I always wonder how people can talk themselves into spending thousands of dollars on nursery gear that will only be needed for two years max. It's sure not for the kid. He'd be just as happy in a drawer. Here's all one actually needs as a new parent.

1. somewhere for baby to sleep (crib—Ikea has nice ones for under $100, Pack 'n Play, bassinet, your bed, a cardboard box)

2. something for baby to eat (breast milk or formula and a few months later some cereal and mashed-up fruit and vegetables)

3. something for baby to wear (onesies for the summer; add some layers when it's cold—almost always available as hand-me-downs from a friend or neighbor, by bulk from eBay or from Old Navy, Target, or Children's Place)

4. some way to transport baby (sling, Baby Bjorn, stroller, or car seat—or, you know, your arms)

5. diapers and wipes (unless you go the wacky "elimi-nation communication" route, it's hard to get around this one. You can go for cloth if you'd rather—although recent studies show the environmental impact is the same because of the washing, so you can't go wrong— or right—ecologically.)

A few months in, you may want to add some toys (empty two-liter bottles, paper towel rolls, and pots and pans all work well), some books (*Goodnight Moon* plus a few others), and bigger clothes (see above for sources).

So you can get away with spending next to nothing.

The only major change in your needs is some babysitting

help so you can get out of the house when you need to, whether that's to work or for your own sanity. But again, even if you don't have family or friends who can help, you can eventually work out some kind of trade-off with a fellow parent or share a babysitter.

This doesn't mean you might not want a fancy stroller or a sleek crib or a full-time nanny—just that you don't *need* any of these things.

The Thousand-Dollar Question: What Kind of Stroller Are You?

Attachment parenting gurus advocate carrying your baby against your body, feeding on demand, and plenty of touching. These are all nice things. At least, I found slings incredibly handy. You can actually carry groceries and the baby at the same time, and a lot of babies totally conk out in those things. Meanwhile, high-end strollers dominate the baby-supply aisles.

This means the pressure is there to both (1) have the baby on you twenty-four hours a day and (2) set up the baby in an ergonomic stroller with speakers, four cup holders, and better shocks than your car. It's a little confusing.

Personally, I registered for a $100 Maclaren Volo and my boss gave it to me at my baby shower. I started using it after my baby outgrew the $20 cotton sling I got on eBay and the $5 Baby Bjorn I got off Craigslist and the $50 Jeep carrier I got for free at work. That stroller was a total workhorse, and when the wheels finally wore down to the point where we were basically shooting off sparks with every step, we went into the nearest Babies "R" Us, got an even lighter $65 red Chicco that lasted another year and a half, and only toward the end required duct tape. After that, we got a $17 umbrella stroller from K-mart that's perfectly serviceable.

Oliver has started to like running down the sidewalk, and he's gotten good at stopping at street corners, so we're phasing out the stroller anyway. In other words, yes, I am totally smug about how cheaply I got through the whole stroller thing. Okay, we are responsible for two little strollers in a landfill somewhere. We have no snazzy stroller to hand down to our friends. And we never had a stroller experience I would describe as *fantastic*. There were no cup holders, iPod speakers, or even cozy recline functionality. The latter was sometimes kind of annoying, like when Oliver fell asleep and to keep him from slumping forward we had to tilt the stroller back on two wheels for a whole shopping expedition.

And yet, I have a list of things I'd rather spend $1,000 on: a trip to Florida for baseball spring training, ten pairs of fancy shoes, or Neal's student loan.

But that's just me. I feel the same way about vacuum cleaners, and so have had a series of $100 ones over the years that are not so hot, when probably I should have just gone ahead and gotten one of those superduper $500 ones. I just have never been able to bring myself to spend that much on something so unsexy.

I asked someone who has one of those deluxe strollers why they're worthwhile and was told: "The design is amazing. I love the way it looks and how it maneuvers. The turning radius is incredible. And people don't mind spending a thousand dollars on a really nice bike if they're a biker, and you don't use a bike every day, whereas you use the stroller every day for like three years—more if you have more than one kid."

"But aren't they big and superheavy?" I asked. "What about on the subway, or up and down stairs, or in narrow stores or anything like that where you have to be kind of lean and mean?"

"We have another one, too, a Volo, that we probably use more often."

Aha! I thought.

"But the Bugaboo is still really amazing and when we use it I'm always glad we have it."

Fair enough. Whenever I look at how tiny our apartment is, I'm always glad we don't have one. But it clearly adds a little gear-heady *frisson* to some parents' days, and you can't really put a price on that.

Oh wait, you can. The price is ONE THOUSAND DOLLARS.

The Disgrace That Is the United States's Leave Policy

The Baby Boomers accomplished a lot for women who wanted to work. The Pill made it easier to control our reproductive freedom. Women were free to work alongside men, and to go to college for any subject. And well done! Women now outnumber men at institutions of higher learning.[12] In some major cities, the wage gap has closed.[13] Second Wavers stood behind President Obama in 2009 as he signed the Lilly Ledbetter Fair Pay Act into law.

But for women who want to have babies, what's been accomplished? There's that Clinton-passed law about how most employers can't fire someone for a few months after they have a baby in case they want to return to their jobs.[14] But there's not a whole lot else.

UK mothers often get thirty-nine weeks' paid leave when they have a baby.[15] In the United States, it can be tough to get more than a few weeks off (paid or unpaid) to spend recovering and holding your newborn before it's back to the desk or the factory or wherever you go to bring home a paycheck.

American families who want to have kids are on their own to make it work. And that usually means getting a lot of baby-sitting help or leaving their jobs. Everyone's economics and emotions are different, so some opt for one or the other, but it's usually the lesser of various evils. And whatever choice is made, there is judgment from one side or the other (or, for the lucky few who try to have it all, both!).

If we stay home with the kids, we often feel like the world is passing us by, because parenting still has no status in our culture. "Homemaker" carries a '50s stigma of suppressed ambition and a glass of wine at the stroke of five p.m. Certain career-focused feminist activists can be heard whispering, "After all we did for you . . . you're going to be a *housewife*?"

Staying at home just isn't widely respected, except by people like Dr. Laura Schlessinger, whose book *In Praise of Stay-at-Home Moms* has this loaded statement on its book jacket: "They number in the millions and they are incredibly important to families and to our society, yet they are underappreciated, little respected, and even controversial. Who are they? They are the stay-at-home moms. These are women who know in their hearts that staying home to raise their children is the right choice for the whole family."[16]

Really? For all families? Every time? How about *In Praise of Anyone Who Raises Good Kids Without Losing His or Her Mind*? That's a book I would read.

Meg Wolitzer, author of *The Ten-Year Nap*, a novel featuring stay-at-home mothers, writes

> For a long time, I think I had been somewhat judgmental about women who stayed at home. I went by the easy assumption that someone who worked was by nature more interesting than someone who didn't. But really, I came to see both as I wrote and as I lived in the world: if you are seated at a dinner next to someone who works in marketing at

Revlon, say, will you definitely have a better time than if you were seated next to someone who stays at home?[17]

Those of us who go back to work while our kids are still little, which is most of us (those women who do opt out return in, on average, 2.2 years, according to Sylvia Ann Hewlett), often end up spending less time with our kids than we'd like.[18] That means a nagging sense that we should be elsewhere, a cloud of guilt and constant second-guessing of our choices and a feeling of being trapped.

This is a very vulnerable position to be in, and it's new to us when we have a baby. Nothing prepares you for how much you love your child or for how hard it is to make the addition of a new person into your family a seamless, simple act of addition. There are infinite numbers of people, be they experts, family, or strangers, eager to prey on your vulnerability and sell you on the one true path. Again, this is rarely helpful. What would be helpful is someone saying, "Here is a new job that lets you work flexible hours." Or, "Here is twenty thousand dollars for childcare between now and kindergarten." Or, "Here is a breathtakingly competent au pair who will work for gummy bears."

Instead, the advice is the opposite of reassuring or pragmatic: "You should really be home with your children until they start kindergarten at least; you'll never get this time back!" is the screed on one side; on the other: "If you leave your job for five years, it will be very hard to work your way back up; those résumé gaps are a red flag!"

"The Opt-Out Revolution," a controversial *New York Times* piece by Lisa Belkin from October 2003, stoked the fire around the issue of staying home versus working.[19]

ADA CALHOUN

"Women—specifically, educated professional women— were supposed to achieve like men," Belkin wrote. "Once the barriers came down, once the playing field was leveled, they were supposed to march toward the future and take rightful ownership of the universe, or at the very least, ownership of their half. The women's movement was largely about grabbing a fair share of power—making equal money, standing at the helm in the macho realms of business and government and law. It was about running the world."

But despite women's widely reported educational advances, the world-running doesn't seem to happen: According to Belkin, "Although men and women enter corporate training programs in equal numbers, just 16 percent of corporate officers are women, and only eight companies in the Fortune 500 have female C.E.O.'s. Of 435 members of the House of Representatives, 62 are women; there are 14 women in the 100-member Senate."

She said the workplace has failed women, sure, but the thrust of the article seemed to be that women have abandoned the workplace because they didn't want to deal with the stress of a hard job. Among the reactions to Belkin's article was, why aren't we focusing on why the U.S. workplace is so family-unfriendly rather than portraying stay-at-home mothers as a disappointment?

It is my hope that in the future, every job will include flex-time. Job sharing will be common. A family will be able to make a living on one job between them. The need for health-care won't tether people to jobs they hate. We will all be able to agree that families deserve the right to determine what option works best for them.

One of Oliver's best friends, Ella, is half-Swedish. Her mother, Johanna, is from Sweden and her father is from Florida. They are one of the hardest-working couples I know. He does sixty-hour weeks. She takes care of Ella all day, every day, while eking out whatever work she can (she's an artist and sound designer). The two of them managed to buy and renovate a three-story building in their spare time and were able to sell it for a big profit even in a bad economy. But she and her husband never have time to do their own work. Ella rarely gets to see her dad. Johanna is burned out and artistically frustrated.

I saw Johanna's studio. There are beautiful ink drawings hanging on the wall in various states of completion. Next to her workstation is a workstation for Ella with a bunch of Play-Doh. The only way Johanna can create is to provide nearby distractions for her toddler. And this means she never knows how long she can work for: An hour? Five minutes? On any given day, how into making Play-Doh spaghetti is Ella? How can you create under those conditions?

So they're moving to Sweden. They will have free healthcare and school and help from Johanna's family, and they won't have to make nearly as much money to have a decent standard of living as they do in New York City. We're going to miss them so much, and I can't imagine leaving the United States myself, but I would move, too, if I were them.

How sad is it that the only way a wonderful, hardworking family like them can achieve work-home balance is to move thousands of miles away?

How We Think About Work

One morning a guy I know ended a game with his son and said he had to go to work. "Why?" his son asked. "To make money," the father said. His son went into his own bedroom, brought out his piggy bank, and said, "Here, Daddy. Now you don't have to go to work."

I think about that on mornings when my son asks why I'm going to the office. I don't mention money. "It's my job," I say. "People are counting on me to be there."

When he asks why he has to go to school, I say the same thing: "It's your job. Miss Rachel's expecting you, and your friends are, too. Benji and Dylan E. and Liberty will all be sad if you're not there. You need to go play with them."

Weirdly, just talking about work and school like that makes me feel better about it. If it's just for money, it feels depressing. It does seem like there should be a way around that—a piggy bank or something—so the family never has to be apart.

But of course money's not only what work is about. You could do a million different things to make enough money to keep the roof over your family's head. You're doing what you're doing, one hopes, because you're suited to it. And even if not, it's what you're doing right now, and what you're doing right now matters. Everyone has things they need to do: brush their teeth, eat and sleep, use the bathroom. Whether or not you *want* to is immaterial. It's what makes up the day.

In a 2009 interview, the actress Julianne Moore said, "I think it's imperative that kids understand that parents have to work for a living, that there's an economic model that you have to follow, which is that you do some work and that enables you to take care of your family, and with any luck you do work that you really enjoy, too. That's the truth of the world. And kids understand that."[20]

I like that idea. It's what you've chosen to do to take care of your family. I also like that it's about responsibility rather than money. My boss and coworkers are expecting me to come in to work. I have writers who need me to edit and publish their work. I have editors who I need to file to. As much as I miss Oliver when I leave the house, there are other people counting on me, too.

We all owe things to other people. Everyone in a community owes things to everyone else. We depend on the guys at the deli to show up for work so we can buy milk and juice and chocolate from them. We need the firemen to show up so if a fire breaks out they can go put it out, and so we can visit the firehouse and sit on the truck.

Children have a job to do, too, a hard job. They have to grow up and learn. They have to eat and sleep. They have to respect their parents. They have to obey rules. And they have to let us take care of them—as well as we possibly can.

The Truth About Cats and Dogs and Babies

There is for sale (and this is true) a CD of baby noises marketed toward expectant parents who own pets. The marketers of this CD encourage you to play it for your pets in order to prepare them for a baby entering their domain. More than one major parenting book encourages you to walk a *baby doll* in a *stroller* when you walk your dog.

As if these things are (a) rational or (b) remotely simulate bringing a human being you love more than life itself into the presence of your formerly favorite creature! It's as if carting a blow-up doll around or playing sultry cabaret music will prepare your wife for when you move your new lounge-singer girlfriend into the marital bed.

Oliver and our cat, Trouble, are friends. Oliver likes to feed Trouble, and to use him as a pillow, and Trouble seems perfectly happy about those things. They both like hanging out in his little kid-size Peapod travel tent (which is the same size as all the available floor space in his room).

Occasionally they'll have a flare-up. When Oliver was six or so months old, he grabbed Trouble's tail and Trouble swatted him on the face. Oliver still has a scar. No one else can see it, but I can—just a tiny line along his cheek, a reminder that we stupidly left the cat and baby alone together on the bed one morning.

The key to having them get along seems to be for us to have zero tolerance for any mistreatment, be that by the animal or by the baby. Neal chased Trouble all over the house after the scratching incident. Almost from birth we've been training Oliver to pet Trouble gently, to talk to him sweetly, to give him his own space. And now not only does he pet the cat lovingly, but he also says things like "Good job, kitty!" when the cat uses the litter box.

We have a remarkably gentle kid and a remarkably patient cat. Not everyone is so lucky. I fully understand why people get rid of their animals when they have a baby. The hard truth is that no one loves their pet as much as they love their kid. You think you understand love when you have a pet, but then a baby comes along and makes you realize how clueless you were before.

"They're like our children," people often say about their pets.[21] I used to think of my cats that way. I took too many photos of them. When family members called to catch up, they would ask of the cats, "How are the kids?" I thought nothing of making sacrifices for their welfare. When our very old cat, Leon, got diabetes a few years ago, Neal and I gave him insulin shots twice a day until he died some months later.

Since we've had a baby, I've started to see things differently. From the moment they handed my son to me in the hospital, I realized the vast difference between an animal being your child and being *like* your child.

Medical emergencies throw this difference into stark relief. If our son, God forbid, needed some astronomically expensive healthcare, I would sell all our possessions, take on five jobs, max out every credit card in sight. I would do anything to save him, up to and including laying down my own life. But I wouldn't do that much for my cat. Unlike my love for my child, my love for my cat isn't unconditional. I adore him, but he's no longer my "kid."

Blogs and Confessions

In an April 2009 article on page A1 of the *Wall Street Journal*, "Bad Parents and Proud of It: Moms and a Dad Confess," the journalist Ellen Gamerman wrote

> *Critiquing other people's parenting has become a sport for many mothers and fathers, aided by the Internet and the sheer volume of available expert advice. Now some parents, hoping to quiet the chorus of opinions, judgments and criticism, are defiantly confessing to their own "bad parenting" moments.*[22]

She'd interviewed me at length for the story. I told her I thought the designation was funny; everyone who makes any decision is a "bad parent" by someone's estimation, because parenting choices are so loaded these days. That's why I think those columns are so popular and provide such a good service: calling oneself a "bad parent" is cathartic and properly, intelligently presented, each essay provokes great conversations about "bad" choices, like keeping kids out of school until age six or letting your kids taste wine or bribing your kids with candy.

The journalist called a bunch of my writers and asked them if they regretted their "confessions," or if they were ashamed.

"If I thought it was really wrong, I wouldn't have *done it* to my kid!" retorted one writer who has written about letting her kid watch a lot of TV.

The reporter even asked me this question: "Do you do background checks on your 'Bad Parent' writers, to make sure they aren't actually abusive?"

First of all, why would a loving mother explaining why she chooses not to use a baby monitor for the good of her family's evenings and her children's sleep be a candidate for Social Services by any standard?

Second of all, *WHAT?!*

Rebecca Traister wrote a May 2009 article for Salon.com called "The Worst Parents in the World," in which she described the current state of parenting writing:

> [American parents] are finally rebelling against the judgments and assumptions and expectations and slings and Bjorns and blogs that get hurled at them while they are "parenting," the term that has, in recent years, come to indicate a full-time, harshly judged, cutthroat vocation, rather than simply something that some adults do partway through their lives.[23]

Some writers have been in this phase for a while. Ayelet Waldman has built a career out of shocking her readers with revelations like loving her husband more than her children or deciding to have a second-trimester abortion when she learned her baby had a genetic abnormality. She doesn't usually provoke the cries of "Yes! Thank you so much for writing this!" the way so many parenting blogs do. She doesn't inspire so much identification as alarm. Like Caitlin Flanagan on the aggressively good-parent front, she's a fire starter.

In a 2003 Salon article called "Navel-Gazing Their Way Through Parenthood," Katie Allison Granju wrote

> *Despite our pop cultural literacy, in one way, we Gen X parents are exactly the same as those who have parented before us; no matter how much we talk, read, write, and think about our own parenting, we won't be able to get a clear picture of what we did right and where we went wrong until our own offspring are grown and can tell us—and their therapists.*[24]

The truth? Most parenting "confessions" are little more than innocent yammering. Chosen at random, here are two mommy bloggers' thoughts on a lovely day in April: "Oooo, I just found these online! Wonder if I could get them here before next Saturday's flight to Florida? My boys LOVE to doodle and I thought this would be an awesome boredom buster for their backpacks bound for the airplane . . ."

And "I left my cell phone charging in my car all day yesterday and when I finally checked it, on the way to Rhyse's 5:30 soccer game, I noticed that Rheumatology called me TWICE. I tried to ring back but the office had closed for the day . . ."

The Internet provides a kind of virtual backyard fence, and everyone's talking to one another about everything they're facing, whether mundane or controversial, heartwarming or desperate. Surely, company when you're going through something as challenging and awe-inspiring as raising children isn't a bad thing?

And yet, there is a weird echo effect in these blogs. There isn't really that much diversity of perspective. The "badness" is pretty predictable most of the time: lying to secure alone-time, having a cocktail at a playdate—in short, occasionally putting yourself first.

But as Kara Jesella points out in an April 2009 article for *The American Prospect,*

> *It's hard to deny the vast gulf between the stay-at-home mom who feels mild guilt when she serves the occasional microwave dinner to her kids and the single mother with two jobs whose kids come home to an empty house and frozen dinners most nights. But those working-class moms aren't blogging several times a day—or at all. And so the self-christened "bad mommies" remain largely unconcerned with the class divide.*[25]

Basically, there is a huge divide between "bad parenting" (having selfish moments or naughty habits) and bad parenting, which means being abusive, neglectful, or cruel. Genuinely bad parenting is a societal problem abetted by limited options. In a sense, "bad parents" are like dilettantes.

Hearing about genuinely bad parenting is depressing. I feel so sorry for those families. I want to help the kids. But hearing about "bad parenting" is fun. It's a nice hit of schadenfreude, and it's frequently inspiring: "I may be bad, but at least I don't do *that.*"

TV or Not TV?

On days when I work at home, the TV is often on for at least a couple of hours of my eight-hour workday, and this was the case even before my son turned two. (The American Academy of Pediatrics in 1999 recommended that children under two watch no TV at all.) Some days, Oliver and I watch a full-length movie or two—him sitting on the bed with a bowl of banana slices, me next to him with my laptop on my lap and a cup of coffee balanced behind me on the windowsill.

His favorites at the moment: *Ratatouille, Cinderella, Wonder Pets*, and a crazy film my Norwegian cousin sent us called *Venner for Livet*. We have gone through phases of *Follow That Bird, Don't Eat the Pictures, Big Bird in China, Old School Sesame Street, Thomas the Tank Engine, The Backyardigans, Beauty and the Beast, Faerie Tale Theatre, Pee-wee's Playhouse*, Scholastic animated books, *Yo Gabba Gabba!*, and *Charlie and Lola*. We memorize our favorite lines and quote them often.

When we are having a bad time someplace, Neal and I say, "This was great. Thanks so much. But I'm WALKING BACK to Sesame Street," as Big Bird does when he's fed up with the Dodo family, whom he's sent to live with in *Follow That Bird*.

When Oliver says, "No! No! No!" we can usually get him laughing by acting out the scene from *Singin' in the Rain*, in which the record and movie go out of sync and the yeses and no's get mixed up.

Movies or DVDs of TV shows that Neal and I hate get "lost," and eventually Oliver forgets about them. Sorry, Casper.

So it's something we do together for the most part, or something we can let him do while we work or take showers. "Did Lola find Sizzles yet?" we can inquire upon returning. Or, "Did the Wonder Pets save the blowfish?" I don't see that it's so much different than reading books together, which we also do a lot of, or than having adventures together in the city, or running around at the playground, which we do every day.

And even on days when we have the TV on a lot and I start to feel like it's too much, I recall that it's still a hell of a lot less TV than I watched as a little kid. I remember a summer in which I did little but watch marathons of *Scooby-Doo*. When I was about ten, I got a mini-TV in my room and would eat my dinner there watching my shows while my parents ate their dinner in the living room while watching their own programming. Sometimes we even watched the same show, although more often I was watching *Benson* while they were watching the news and discussing Reagan.

I am not alone. Generation X was the first generation to have color television in its homes from the start.[26] We logged many, many, many hours in front of the tube, and it shows in our obsession with pop culture, our cartoon-derived sense of humor, and our famously weak attention span. So it's no wonder that we have really mixed-up feelings about how much TV our own kids should watch.

The journalist L. J. Williamson writes, "Parents haven't totally ignored the anti-TV warnings from pediatricians; we've just assimilated them into our consciousness as we simultaneously violate them. The result is a nagging background noise of guilt competing with the background noise of the tube. Nearly every parent I've spoken to allows his or her child to watch TV, and nearly every parent has misgivings about it. We're holding a remote in one hand, and a burden of guilt in the other."[27]

Some parents have rebelled against the television, banning it altogether from their homes. Of course, there's still the computer. Ironically, some parents of our generation have "Kill Your TV" bumper stickers but will let their toddlers watch three straight hours of kittens riding Roombas, *C Is for Cookie*, and locomotives chugging into stations on YouTube.

A good friend of mine doesn't have a TV at all. She lets her kids watch DVDs, but there's no television in the house. "It's as much to keep myself from zoning out in front of it as anything," she says. But clearly it's had a profound effect on her children. They are extremely precocious, have ridiculously long attention spans, and are freakishly creative. They write plays and act them out. They write thank-you notes! They are a walking ad for no-TV.

I'm still not getting rid of ours, though. I need my daily dose of Anderson Cooper, so I'm not going to begrudge Oliver the occasional episode of *Diego*.

Scary Stories

Today's children's books invariably treat children's psyches as hopelessly fragile. This may or may not be a good thing. Even if Grimm's fairy tales, with all their decapitations and serial wife murders, don't seem appropriate for toddlers, maybe neither is a steady diet of sanitized, scare-free pabulum.

According to an article by Liza Featherstone called "Be Afraid, Be Very Afraid," scary stories have a psychological benefit.[28] "By requesting the same alarming story over and over, a child is mastering his fears about death, punishment, and scary animals, all of which are part of real life. Scary books are a kind of play therapy. 'The importance of bad things in stories is that they help create pretend space where bad things can happen,' says Dr. Tony Charuvastra, a research psychiatrist at NYU School of Medicine's Child Study Center. It helps them process their feelings of anxiety, and to act out their fears in their imagination before they face them in the real world."

I've started to wonder, though, if there isn't a significant difference between books and movies—namely, in how freaked out kids are by scary scenes in books versus in movies. Neal is all for Oliver watching *The Wizard of Oz,* but I insist he fast-forward through the flying monkeys, because those *still* freak me out, and I've seen *Dawn of the Dead* multiple times.

Ken Kwapis, director of the classic 1985 film *Follow That Bird*, scarred many a child by depicting Big Bird, dyed blue and weeping, trapped in a sideshow cage by malicious carnies. I asked Kwapis by phone whether or not he'd felt conflicted about showing such a brutal image to little kids.[29] (Oliver, age two, was totally fine with it, by the way, but a few people I spoke to who saw the film as kids said it was one of the most traumatic film experiences they can remember.)

Kwapis said, "When I worked on the film, by coincidence, it wasn't like I was using this as part of my preparation, but I read Bruno Bettelheim's book *The Uses of Enchantment* and his general thesis is—and he's writing about reading, and stories that are told to one another—that each child will imagine what they're able to tolerate. That's why *Hansel and Gretel* to a three-year-old or four-year-old is tolerable, because they will imagine as much as they're capable of tolerating.

"The difficulty with films is that an image can strip your gears as a child and run roughshod over your ability to keep things in check. And that's why *Pinocchio* is famously difficult for some children. When Pinocchio's pal on Pleasure Island metamorphoses into a donkey, it is seen as a shadow on the wall, so even they had the good sense to imply the horror and not to show it so directly."

One rainy day Oliver and I were sitting on my bed watching *Cinderella*, which he'd picked out at the movie store (it being his adored cousin's favorite film). Oliver was enjoying it to no end. He laughed at the mice and the cat and smiled as Cinderella sang songs while cleaning the floor. He was enraptured. When Cinderella wafted down the stairs in the pink dress her rodent friends have sewed for her, he cheered. But then when Cinderella's stepsisters started tearing at her dress,

Oliver's face scrunched up, his mouth turned down, and tears sprang from his eyes. He started sobbing.

I grabbed him up in my arms and held him tight, talking as reassuringly as I could: "She's going to be okay! It's all going to be fine! The mean, mean sisters tore her dress, but she's going to find a way to get to the ball! You'll see! Just watch and you'll see; her fairy godmother is coming!"

Oliver looked up from my shoulder and saw Cinderella crying in the woods. *"Waaaaaaaaaaaaaaaaaaaah!"* he screamed, burying his face back in the crook of my neck. "Look, it's the fairy godmother! Look!" I called, as desperate as Cinderella's own mice friends at this point for the plot to turn around. Oliver looked up, watched as the fairy godmother arrived, worked her magic, and sent Cinderella off to the ball. Oliver smiled and went back to watching happily. "They're dancing!" he said, cheery but still tearstained, when Cinderella hooked up with the prince.

I felt awful, like I should have spared him that moment of pain. But then I thought it might not be so bad for him after all. Stories are a way for us to act out disappointment in short little bursts so that when it hits us for real later, it's not such a shock. And Oliver demanded to watch it again the next day and when the scary part was coming, he said, "Here comes the scary part!" And then, "Ooh, they're so mean!"

A girl I used to babysit for says that when she was Oliver's age she thought that what happened in the Disney films actually was happening in real life—like in a box or something. It was not a movie for her. It was real.

I hope Oliver's old enough now that he knows those horrible sisters aren't really destroying Cinderella's gown over and over again, but maybe it doesn't matter. Maybe the feelings are real and that's all that counts. And a feeling of empathy for a good girl in a bad situation seems like an appropriate response. He's upset by injustice wherever he finds it, even in the movies, and I can live with that.

So we'll keep watching the movies, only we'll keep watching them together and talking about them, and I'll keep in mind how real they are for him when I'm picking out DVDs at the movie store (which Oliver still unfortunately pronounces "boobie store," as in: "Mama, I want to see a *boobie*!").

For as long as he's seeing the world in a relatively nuance-free way, I don't want him seeing movies in which evil triumphs, or in which the good-hearted hero or heroine doesn't end up madly in love and living in a castle. That's a rough analogy of what I want for him: true love and a happy home. I believe it's possible, and I'm sure not going to show him movies that tell him it isn't.

Travels with Baby

I have a travel tip! I didn't think I would ever be able to give someone else tip-style advice about anything, but now I do, and here it is: On your first full day in a new town where you will be spending more than a couple of days, go directly to the nearest thrift store. Go to the toy department and buy the most badass toy there. It will typically cost less than five dollars, and it will give your child something awesome to play with when he's bored, and something that's all his in an anonymous new place. Also, unless you routinely buy your child fancy presents, it will feel really luxurious to waltz in and plunk down a few dollars for something that would usually cost ten times more.

When we went to Florida in March, we visited the Golden Rule Academy Thrift Shop and bought a red, plastic, sit-in pedal-car for $3.50 (also purchased: new Timberland boots, size 9-Toddler for $3.99). We took our find back to the hotel, set it down on the pathway leading to the pool area, and watched as Oliver propelled himself slowly but steadily around and around on the concrete and grass for a solid hour before even looking up.

He was in heaven. We grown-ups got to chat in the Florida sunshine. By the end of the trip, that little plastic car had given Oliver happy memories, great exercise, and a very cool vantage point from which he could talk to our fellow guests and survey the palm trees.

I am a firm believer in value. And that car paid for itself a hundred times over.

When we left, I said we wouldn't be allowed to bring it on the plane, and suggested we give it to the little girl in the next room over. Oliver seemed okay with that and he showed it off to her like a car salesman. He climbed in and drove it past her while talking about it; he showed how the horn worked. Then he climbed out and said, happily, "Now you try it!"

She got in and beamed. Oliver and I carried our suitcases to the car and drove off toward the airport. "Wait!" he said suddenly. "Where's my car?" "We gave it to that little girl, remember?" I asked. "We couldn't take it on the plane and so we left it at the hotel."

"I need my car!" he wailed.

Suddenly I felt like a total idiot. Oh, good one; give him an awesome toy but make him *give it away* after three days? What kind of a stupid parent was I?

Luckily, by the time we got to the airport, he seemed to have totally forgotten it, and when he looks at photos of the trip, the car is just one more piece of scenery that he recalls fondly, like the sand castles on the beach or the pool.

Of course, watch as that abandoned red car haunts him forever.

So I take it back; I have no advice, unless it's to make all cool trip gifts travel-size. I will probably continue to gamble with my son's psyche by getting him vacation vehicles, but I do so with some hesitation and with the knowledge that I may in fact be scarring him for life. Bon voyage!

Marital Relations

I recently saw some scary quiz results online:

How often do you argue with your spouse about who does what?

Constantly. / Sometimes. / Never.[30]

I thought "Sometimes" was a lock. In fact: 90 percent said "Constantly."

Really? What is going on? How do people live like that?

It really freaked me out, because I tend to give my generation (I was born in 1976) so much credit for getting past the old Mars-Venus resentments, strict gender roles, and all the hostility that goes along with them.

For me, the difference between our kind of marriage and our parents' kind of marriage really hit home during the 2008 presidential primary campaign. My mother came over one morning and said, "Well, I'm off Hillary."[31]

This was shocking. From the first, she's been a die-hard Hillary supporter. Loved Bill, *loved* Hillary. Even as my father became an Obama fan, my mother stuck by the Clintons.

What changed her mind? Bill. "Why doesn't she send him to Iceland?" my mother asked of Hillary, furious. "Why doesn't he let her have her turn? It's so like the men of our generation. He's out to sabotage her."

She's not the first to notice how in the name of support Bill has tended to undermine his wife. The *New York Times* ran a rather snide story in May 2006 about the Clintons' marriage: "Mr. Clinton is rarely without company in public, yet the company he keeps rarely includes his wife."[32]

But even the worst insinuations in that piece weren't as bad as the truth: the Clintons have an absolutely typical Boomer union, a rickety first-generation prototype of the modern marriage. They were early adopters of this "equal partnership" thing, so while they deserve all credit for having pioneered, their marriage is the romantic equivalent of the Apple IIe.

The Boomer marriage has a lot of things that got phased out in later development. They're trying hard to be good at mutual respect and encouragement, but there's only so far you can upgrade an old machine.

So the Clintons proclaim and demonstrate their love, convincingly: "No one understands me better and no one can make me laugh the way Bill does," Hillary wrote in her 2003 memoir. "He's so romantic!" she cooed to *Essence*. He kisses her on the forehead. They hug. I totally buy it. And then, like clockwork, he screws her over. She seethes, reasserts her independence. They make up. Rinse and repeat.

Contrast that with the Obamas. Their marriage looks progressive, fair, and fun. That's not to say they don't probably fight plenty, but there's something remarkably bitterness-free about them. They seem to genuinely enjoy each other and they seem like a team. The Clintons seem like two strong oxen yoked together and not always wanting to go in the same direction. And judging by how young men and women relate to each other these days, the Obamas' notion of partnership looks more like the future.

There is still plenty of the Boomer relationship ethos around. In 2009 the journalist Michael Lewis (born in 1960) published *Home Game*, a parenting memoir that expresses contempt for how much work he's expected to do to raise his children.

Here's one passage:

> *At some point in the last few decades, the American male sat down at the negotiating table with the American female and—let us be frank—got fleeced. The agreement he signed foisted all sorts of new paternal responsibilities on him and gave him nothing of what he might have expected in return . . . Not even the admiration of the body politic, who pushed him into signing the deal . . . The world looks at him schlepping and fetching and sagging and moaning beneath his new burdens and thinks: OH . . . YOU . . . POOR . . . BASTARD.*

"Oh my God!" my friend Tara said when I read that to her. "That is gross and so not true! When I see a man who's involved with his kids I think he's hot! Everyone does. Maybe fifty years ago it had some kind of stigma, but today it's cool to be an involved father."

I asked a few Gen X fathers I know if that was true to their experience and they were appalled by how cynical Lewis seemed. "What a poser," one said of Lewis. "What does his wife think of that book? If my wife ever wrote anything like that about me and our kids, I'd divorce her ass."

On the playgrounds of America, men are sharing the care

of their children and even seeming to enjoy it. Men and women are seeking increasingly flexible schedules so that they can spend more time with their families. According to a 2007 *Newsweek* article, "between 1985 and 2003 the amount of time men spent on child care rose from 2.6 hours to 7 hours per week."[33] A 1996 poll by the same magazine found "seven out of 10 American fathers spend more time with their children than their own fathers did."[34] Daddy diaper bags abound.

And yet, looking around, I have to admit, even among my Generation X peers, there is plenty of old-fashioned heterosexual strife.

Despite how much more involved men are these days, women still put in twice as many hours as men. According to University of Maryland sociologist Suzanne Bianchi, quoted in the 2007 *Newsweek* piece mentioned above, "If anyone drops out of the labor force, it's usually the moms. If anyone cuts back to part-time, it's more often moms. And dads who work full-time work: 45 to 50 hours per week to a mother's 35 or 40 hours."

The Nation writer Katha Pollitt has said that parenthood turns even the most equitable couples into "gender Republicans."[35] In other words, after the birth of her child, "The old assumptions about men and women, which had been lulled by money and leisure and youthful bohemianism and feminism, woke up."

"I think there may be a little more gender flexibility in the social class where incomes between men and women are more equal," Pollitt told me over drinks one evening in New York.[36] "But when there's a banker married to a would-be folk singer, I don't think the banker is taking six months off to stay home with the baby."

In fact, in many of the happier marriages I know about, the men make less money than the women. Rhona Mahony suggests in her book *Kidding Ourselves: Breadwinning, Babies, and Bargaining Power* that women who want kids and a career should marry down. That makes a lot of sense to me. One of the partners should probably be responsible for home if the other is going to work a lot, and so if you want to work a lot you should find someone who's a homebody. At least until we get reasonable workplace reform.

Pollitt says that regardless of which path you choose, "I think it's probably a good idea to think it out before you have the baby. Often, the woman just assumes, 'Oh, I'll just have the baby and we'll have some babysitters and it'll all be the same.' But it's not going to be all the same, because children take a lot more time than you think they're going to and they have a lot of needs that are hard to plan for."

Even couples I know who've gotten beyond problems like that have issues. One problem is a lack of support from their friends. A working mother I know is regularly told by friends and strangers that her husband must feel emasculated by her breadwinning, and must hate spending so much time with their young son rather than being "out in the world."

I was lucky to marry a man who happens to be home a lot during the day. Because he's a performer, he just works a couple of nights a week, other than during rehearsals or auditions.

Still, it's easy to get bitter if you let it happen. When I was working and breastfeeding (or pumping the two days a week I was in the office), I got bitter. I figured I was doing at least 75 percent of the work involved in taking care of our baby, even though my husband was staying home with him. Of course, my husband thought he was doing 75 percent, too, because on the days I went into the office, he had hours and hours of monotonous time rocking the baby in the rocking chair and listening to playlist after playlist. Plus, he cleaned and cooked and was trying to keep his own career going.

My conclusion: as soon as you have a baby, there is at least 200 percent more stuff to do. There is always more than you think, and the other person is probably doing a lot of work you don't notice, like getting milk on the way home or waking up at night to check on a coughing child or picking socks up off the floor.

According to *What Predicts Divorce?: The Relationship Between Marital Processes and Marital Outcomes* by John Mordechai Gottman, "Complaining and criticism leads to contempt, which leads to defensiveness, which leads to listener withdrawal from interaction (stonewalling)." These marital behaviors he calls, rather dramatically, "The Four Horsemen of the Apocalypse."[37]

The secret seems to be reducing stress as much as possible.

That means letting go of anything that's not urgent. Forget about a clean house. Order a lot of takeout. Get babysitters just so you can go walk around together out of the house. Don't give up on sex. And just try really hard to be nice and generous even though it's superhard to not feel overwhelmed. Everyone feels that way for at least part of her kids' early years. But it's so much easier if you have someone on your team.

Those First Weeks
Back from Leave

Giving a coworker directions to our home shortly after I'd gone back to work, I said, "From the office, it's about thirty minutes, door to door."

What I was thinking was, *If you race down the stairs rather than wait for the slow elevator, make all the walk lights to the subway, get off at the very back of the train, and run down the stairs past the old ladies, then cross past the construction site and jog the last block, you can make it in twenty.*[38]

And for the first few weeks or months after I returned to the office, that was my personal approach to work-home balance: efficiency bordering on OCD.

A doctor I know is the worst nightmare of suddenly-everywhere writers like Leslie Bennetts, whose 2007 book, *The Feminine Mistake*, criticizes educated women for opting out of the workplace. Of course, the choice is not as simple as pundits like Bennetts make it sound.

The doctor-mom says,

We are the generation that took pride in the fact that we could break the glass ceiling or devote our lives to our children; society would accept anything. But it won't. It's very difficult to work overnights when you're breastfeeding. There's always pressure to work more. So we have to give up something. And if you're an educated woman, that usually means neglecting your kids or your career, and feeling guilty either way.[39]

One of the hardest things we're all doing is figuring out how to balance work and home. We can't be with our kids full-time and doing whatever else we love full-time, too. So how much of either do we sacrifice?

Pamela Stone, the author of *Opting Out?: Why Women Really Quit Careers and Head Home,* is one of the few authors asking women why they made the choices they have rather than attacking them for either working too much or too little. Her conclusion: the lack of flexible work options is making it impossible, or at least extremely difficult, for women to have it all.

Stone says,

Bankers used to have what were called banker's hours, because they were good hours. Well, a banker's hours are horrible hours now. All these professions are going into a speed-up at the same time that you have more women with family responsibilities. So there is this head-on collision of these two trends.[40]

During these early weeks and months, on the way to work I would trudge to the subway, lugging my briefcase and my pump bag, having bid farewell to a baby who was usually mad at me for leaving and a husband who was gearing up for a lonely day sitting in the rocking chair holding our small boy for hours on end.

I would put in a long day, during which I would mostly be fulfilled, but also periodically annoyed, undermined, and irritable. I had to pump every couple of hours, sitting in the bathroom, listening to the *ka-chunk, ka-chunk, ka-chunk* of my comically named Pump In Style. Ah yes, *Style*—code word for "the little bathroom with the electrical outlet."

I had decadently spent the extra $20 for the cute "limited edition" pump bag—blue with brown piping—and so it looked more like an overnight bag than a contraption. "Going to the Catskills?" a coworker asked me when she saw me carrying it. And thus a new euphemism was born. Every time I headed to the bathroom, I would say, "Off to the Catskills. Back in fifteen."

Neal would bring Oliver by once a day so I could nurse him. They seemed like they were having so much fun. I knew it was hard, what Neal was doing, but compared to the stress of work and the Catskills visits and the missing my baby, it seemed pretty enviable. They would go to the zoo or to the museum or to the park or hang out at the house listening to music while I would have meetings and field e-mails and make up schedules and edit stories.

I was jealous of their time together, and their freedom to do whatever they wanted all day. If I got home and there was nothing in the house for dinner and I had to take the initiative to call for a pizza, I got grouchy. Couldn't they have gone to the grocery store and gotten some stuff for tacos? I'd had five meetings, fired two bloggers, received two hundred e-mails, and made a dozen executive decisions; couldn't Neal have bought a couple of Hungry Man frozen dinners?

Sure, my being at work was worth it: I was making enough money for us to live pretty well. I was confident I was doing something that was good for the culture and for my career. But on the harder days, I envied what I imagined was a blissful domestic scene, a literal walk in the park. And the worst part was not really feeling like I had a choice. I was the one with the best way to make money right now, so I had to make the money. I would probably be stir-crazy at home.

But that didn't stop me from fantasizing: *If I were the one at home, I would not only be locked in a day-long embrace with my child; I also would organize our drawers! I would bake cookies! I would catch up with friends while Oliver cooed at them across the café table.*

The more annoying my workday was, the more bucolic I imagined home was—and the more irritated I was when I arrived home and found the house a mess and heard tales of how Oliver hadn't taken a morning nap and was cranky or how Neal was exhausted.

He was exhausted? *I* was exhausted. *I* was doing the hard work. And I was missing out on a good thirty hours a week of time with my new baby. Plus, I was pumping breast milk every couple of hours to keep the baby alive! Top that!

Of course, this sense of being unappreciated—minus the breast milk bit—is what men used to feel all the time. (To be fair, '50s men had the added onus of wearing three-piece suits and hats in the summer, whereas I could roll into the office wearing a miniskirt, a T-shirt, and pink sneakers.) "Where's my dinner?" they would boom upon their return. I could so relate.

Meanwhile, my husband was home taking care of Oliver, and feeling what many pre–*Feminine Mystique* women used to feel all the time: bored, lonely, and desperate. He would go days without talking to another grown-up except for me on the phone, and I was often busy, so when he called me, I would get off the line quickly. Oliver needed constant attention: diaper changes, bottles of pumped milk, tedious feedings of cereal or mashed bananas, lots of hanging out in the rocking chair or walking around the neighborhood trying to find something to do that would be fun for both a thirty-one-year-old man and a six-month-old baby.

Almost none of our friends had babies, or were married yet. (When we go to visit Neal's family in Texas, they are amazed I was able to conceive at the ripe old age of twenty-nine, but in New York we were, at thirty and thirty-one, among the youngest parents at the playground.) And some of our friends turned out to be not all that comfortable with babies. If the baby cried, they would freak out. And yet, if the baby cooed at them, they looked away. It's kind of hard not to take personally disregard for one's adorable infant, so that wound up being a deal-breaker for some friends.

To add insult to injury, Neal was often second-guessed by old ladies in the neighborhood. He'd be walking around chatting away to Oliver in the sling or stroller and be yelled at for not having a hat on the baby (during a heat wave). Sure, some hot girls would make eyes at him or squeal over how cute the baby was. But perks such as that were undone by the middle-aged ladies who would coo about how Daddy was "babysitting." (For the record, fathers don't babysit; they parent, just like mothers do.)[41]

Arguably, our situation was better than the traditional model, because at least we'd ostensibly chosen our roles. I liked my job, so I went to work. Neal was already at home a good part of the week, so he just stayed there when the baby came. Easy, right?

Sadly, no. As enlightened and progressive as we were, we still had some expectations embedded in our subconscious of what men and women should do. Neal felt a little emasculated that I was earning all the money. I heard it in his voice when we met someone at a party and was asked what he did. He would say "Performance artist" and when someone asked how he made a living doing that he would say, defensively, "I do okay."

I felt, on occasion, like a bad mother. If I left home and arrived back to a sleeping baby, I would worry that Oliver would forget me, that I would become nothing more than a means of support (and milk). I imagined Oliver and his father in a bubble of love, and me saying, "Um, remember me?" to a blinking little boy.

So in those early weeks when I got home from the office, I would try to do everything a mother should: I bathed Oliver and sang to him. When he was asleep, I cleaned the bathroom. I baked and froze lasagnas. I sorted through Oliver's clothes and boxed up hand-me-downs to send to his cousin. And sometimes I would go a little overboard with all the mothering, scrubbing the tub and rearranging the kitchen cabinets to optimize the household management when I should have been spending time with Neal and taking a break long enough to watch TV.

I was working myself into the ground trying to control things even when I wasn't there. *Every time they reach into this cabinet of sippy cups, they will think of me, for I have cleaned and arranged them so the lids will not fall behind the stove! When they are on the subway, they will reach into the diaper bag I have packed and there shall be extra toys! I will have averted a tantrum even though I'm not there! I am amazing!*

One friend of mine and her husband have fallen into a very traditional model of marriage and parenting: he goes off each morning with his briefcase to a high-powered job; she stays at home with the kids and tries to eke out some work (she's a freelancer) during their naps or TV time. ("We watch at least one full-length movie a day; that's all I'm going to say," she confided to me.) They put the kids in daycare a couple of days a week so she can go to her part-time job, which involves a long commute. She arrives home exhausted after picking up the kids and still is somehow responsible for making dinner.

When her husband gets home, all he wants to do is zone out in front of the TV. And that's understandable, because he is wiped out from a hard day's work. But when my friend gets home from her job, all she does is see her husband ignoring her and the kids and the millions of things that need to be done around the house. She comes off feeling like a shrew, but she feels like he's freezing them out. She glares at him when he switches the TV on or when he fails to hear his daughter's request for a sippy cup of apple juice. The marriage gets less fun for both of them by the day.

Inequality is bound up in the arrangement, and the unspoken rules reveal themselves on special occasions like snow days. "Because even if it's a workday for me," my friend says, "guess who's staying home? It would never even occur to him that he should stay home so I could go to work." Because he makes more money and his job is more "important," he's out the door and she's on the phone trying to wrangle childcare or calling her boss to say she can't make it.

The key seems to be that anyone who feels trapped in a role is unhappy regardless of whether that role is stay at home or at work. And it doesn't help that in order to get by financially, couples in the United States generally need at least an income and a half.

The journalist Barbara Ehrenreich in her book *The Hearts of Men: American Dreams and the Flight from Commitment* argues, controversially, that men basically kicked off the women's movement. She says they were so dissatisfied by life as the breadwinner that they opted out of their traditional roles, forcing women to come up with another plan than being supported by their husbands. Ehrenreich notes, "The fact that men marry in precisely the same numbers as women do conceals a basic inequality of motivation: namely, that in the sort of marriage we have rather suddenly come to see as 'traditional,' women need men much more than men need women. Women tried to 'land a man.' Men saw marriage as a 'trap.'"[42]

It was an ugly, stifling bargain for both parties, but men were the ones who, Ehrenreich argues, gave up the game first—walking away from their role as breadwinner.

Today, most people who choose to enter into a marriage do so as equal partners, but society moves slowly, and a lot of the old ideas still linger in our policies and our beer commercials. And our playgrounds.

So many couples today are realizing that a life without balance is pretty miserable. Those who are working want to spend more time with their kids, so they're trying to negotiate part-time work, telecommuting, and paternity or maternity leave. Those who are home want to also have a career of some sort, or at least a social life, so they're picking up freelance work and part-time gigs.

It's a constant challenge figuring out what work is worth what amount of time away from our families and what amount of time with our families is worth what amount of penny-pinching or cabin fever.

When Oliver was a few months old, I was offered a new job that sounded pretty fancy, but it was for a company that I wasn't 100 percent behind. It wasn't doing any good in the world. I could argue that for as fancy an organization as it was, it actually benefited a kind of person that I didn't like. I couldn't really make a case for it being worth time away from Oliver.

My job at Babble had some problems, but I had two days a week at home and at least the hours I spent away from my child seemed to be doing the world some good. Every time I ran an essay that got "thankyouthankyouthankyouthankyou" as feedback, it made me feel like I was doing something positive. I could be reassured by the fact that my time away from home, which amounted to about thirty hours a week (*of which he slept ten!* I reminded myself) actually had value.

I keep that in mind now that I'm still working those hours at the same job, plus more after he goes to sleep. He misses me and I miss him, but it's not ruining him that I'm away from him a few hours three days a week. Plus, when I'm with him I'm really with him. I am forcing myself to turn off my Black-Berry whenever I can and just hang out. And when I'm not with him, he's with people he loves and who love him, usually his father or his grandmother or his magical babysitter or his beloved nursery school teacher.

"I missed you, Mama!" he shouts when I get home, and he throws his arms around me. It kills me. But for every time he complains when I drop him off at school and insists I stay with him, or at least wave to him from the window, there's a day when he doesn't even look back and dives right into a puzzle.

It's hard not to feel a loss missing these hours at home with him, even as necessary as it is for my sanity and our financial well-being. Some days are harder than others. One day when I came home, Neal said Oliver had spent an hour that afternoon playing a game where he saw "Mama" flying above him. He jumped up in the air, caught me from the sky, and dragged me down and hugged me.

Hearing of this imaginative, heartbreaking game, I burst into tears. My little boy, missing his mama so much that he imagined I was floating around on the ceiling and he had to lasso me! How gothic! I imagined his psyche scarred by loneliness, his little fragile ego crushed already by an absentee mother. . . .

"Hey c'mon," Neal said, patting my back. "Don't take it so hard. He plays the same game with Elmo."

Cars and Trucks
and Things That Go

Neal and Oliver and I were walking down the street.

"What's that?" Oliver asked, pointing at a construction site.

"A skid steer," I said, in between sips of coffee.

"How do you know that?" Neal asked, impressed.

"Richard Scarry's *Cars and Trucks and Things That Go*," I said. "Unlike you, I read more than two pages of it."

Neal skips ten or twenty pages at a time of that one. I just hope for his sake that Oliver gets sick of that book before he notices that there has to be something in between the family's visit to the beach and their need for snow tires.

Unlike him, I love all those truck books and that they've taught me the difference between an excavator and a front-end loader. I enjoy the classic DVD *I Dig Dirt*, and get 100 percent every time on the "I Dig Dirt quiz" at the end of the video. "Three hundred sixty feet!" I call out proudly when asked by the TV how long the crane is on Ursa Major, one of the biggest earth-moving machines in the world. The film offers a very romantic portrait of coal mining. Since watching it, I have had dreams of moving to Wyoming and driving a dump truck bigger than a house.

I knew I was super into having a truck-obsessed son when I pointed and enthusiastically yelled, "Cement mixer!" one day on the way home from work, then realized I was all alone (except for some bemused fellow pedestrians standing next to me waiting to cross the street).

"I kept doing that after my son had grown up," a mother I met said. "I kept yelling to my daughter, 'Look, honey! It's a cement mixer! A logging truck! An oil tanker truck!' And my daughter would just stare at me like I was a lunatic."

Some girls totally do get into trucks, too, and plenty of boys prefer tutus and Disney princesses. But a large number of boys love anything with wheels.

And I'm so happy about it! It's totally selfish: I am deeply grateful for an excuse to go by our local firehouse once a week or so. We peek in the window at the trucks, and if someone spots us, the door magically opens. Oliver is whisked in, fitted with a helmet, handed a flashlight, and put up in the truck. He is in heaven—and, chatting with firemen, so am I.

For real, how cute are they? We try to bring by presents regularly. They eat like teenagers, so cookies are always a safe bet. And we stay only a short time, long enough for Oliver to get a fix of fire truck (or fire engine—there is a difference, it turns out) and for me to get close enough to a strapping man in uniform to smell him.

Oliver's beloved babysitter Erica and I are kind of obsessed with these trips to the firehouse. We've started joking that Oliver's going to get sick of going, and we're going to be all, "I have an idea! Let's go to the firehouse today! Come on! I'll buy you a Snickers if you fake excitement over a fire extinguisher."

I understand why people want to give their daughters trucks and their sons dolls. Unisex idealism has a certain nobility. But gender is a spectrum, and most boys are at the truckish end of it. We make sure we have different toys on

hand. Oliver has dolls, too, and enjoys cuddling them and pre-
tending to tuck them into bed. His teacher says the boys in his
class are even more maternal in the play-home area than the
girls. Oliver enjoys the wood dollhouse we got him for Christmas—especially the fake minifood our crafty friend made him
to feed the dolls. But he carries a plastic Tonka fire truck everywhere these days, even sleeps with it.

One day we were out early and a garbage truck pulled up
near us.

"Look, Oliver!" I shouted, and he was duly impressed as we
watched the workers load bags of trash in and compress them.
The worker came over to him and said hi, and showed him the
lever he pulled. I said, "That's a great truck you have there"
(this, by the way, turns out to be a surefire way to get your kid
some time with said truck). He said thank you and showed
some more things about the truck to Oliver.

"He wants to drive one of these someday," I said. "He's obsessed."

"I was, too," the sanitation worker said. "And I never grew
out of it." He looked really happy. And I thought *I would be totally happy if Oliver grew up to drive a trash truck*. Especially if
he took as much pride in his rig as this guy did, and was sweet
enough to show kids how the levers worked. And if he would
give his mother an occasional ride.

Other People's Kids

A friend of mine and I were at the playground talking about the other parents we know. As everyone learns, this is one of the fastest, easiest ways to bond with someone: gossiping about other people. And when it's about parenting, it's even easier as long as you know you're on the same page or you like each other enough to pretend you agree on everything.

"Look at that!" she said as our kids ran squealing from the playground pavement into a little field of grass and leaves. "The other parents are keeping their kids from climbing around on this big pile of sticks that our kids are playing in. They're afraid of dirt! Why are parents today so afraid of dirt?!"

"I know!" I said, nodding vigorously. "And do you see how nicely our kids are sharing that chocolate-chip cookie? Those other parents are feeding their kids, what, tofu crackers? Those kids look so sad!"

"For real! I think junk is such an important part of a kid's life!"

"OMG, me too! I mean—kids have a stressful time of figuring out how the world works! Of course they want to kick back occasionally with a few Oreos and *Dora the Explorer*."

"Totally! I mean, we don't have a TV, but we would watch it a *lot* if we did!"

God love her. That's how you can identify a good playground friend: she goes out of her way to find any similarity she can, even if it's a hypothetical scenario. And she is eager to decry all other parents besides you two, and all other children but yours.

This stage of a parent-parent friendship is almost romantic, when you set yourself in opposition to the rest of the parenting world. Whipped up into a frenzy of superiority over all other parents, everywhere, we almost burst into a rendition of the *West Side Story* anthem, "There's a place for us / Somewhere a place for us."

It takes a few months of going to the park every day or two, but at a point you realize you have an opinion about absolutely everyone. There's the bad kid, the sweet kid, the totally weird kid, the really-good-at-sharing kid, the sociopath. . . .

And the parents! And the nannies! Why does anyone think hanging out at playgrounds gets boring? Not only do you get to hang out with your kid; it's also like watching your very own soap opera unfold one afternoon at a time.

We need friends and our kids need friends and they don't have to be the same people. Usually if you like the kid, you'll like the parents, and vice versa. That's because sane parents often have sane kids. But not always. Sometimes you love the parents and their kid is a monster. Sometimes your kid adores a classmate whose parents you can't stand.

There are a couple of playrooms in our neighborhood. One frigid Saturday the only one open was the one we usually avoided: the expensive one full of bratty kids. But in spite of the $7 grilled cheese and the $5 playground fee, it did its job. After a couple of hours, our son had run himself ragged. He seemed to be hugging his best friend, but really they were

INSTINCTIVE PARENTING • • • 69

holding each other up in order to keep from falling asleep. So I went to get him out of one of the playscapes. A five-year-old boy was yelling at him, "You can't come in here! You're a *baby!*"

When I came over to pick up Oliver, this boy turned to me as if I was going to agree with him and said, "He's a baby! He can't come in here!" I said, "That's rude," and went to retrieve my son, who was obliviously playing. "Are you taking him home?" the rude boy asked. "Yes," I said. "Yes!" he said, making a victory gesture with his arm. "I like it when *babies* go home."

I had to walk away to avoid yelling at him. "Oliver, come along," I said, to no avail. Oliver continued to play, oblivious to the ageism of his horrid playmate.

"It's not working!" the boy yelled after me. "He's not leaving!"

I kept walking away. I went over and sat down with our friends for a second and told them essentially to hold me back.

I couldn't help it. I hated this kid. Hated. You kind of think maybe kids are all fundamentally okay until you're around a lot of them. Then you realize there are some incredibly amazing, cool, and fun kids you'd just as soon adopt. There are a ton of totally fine kids you don't mind your kid finger-painting with once in a while. And then there are the kids who make you rethink your negative feelings about corporal punishment.

They're little people, and some of them inevitably are going to grow up to be the people talking loudly into their cell phones behind you at the post office or cutting in front of a taxi line or making offensive jokes in the break room—the future telemarketers of the world, if you will.

I'm often harder on my kid after I encounter such children. If he shows a hint of jerky behavior, I clamp down. "Uh, did you just nudge your friend out of the way so you could reach your rice cake?! Never nudge! No nudging! Nudging is a gateway to shoving, which is a gateway to being one of those kids who tell their parents to shut up and are abusive to younger children. Don't nudge!"

In a May 2009 MNSBC.com article I was interviewed for, Susan Gregory Thomas wrote

> *By many accounts Generation X may be the most devoted parents in history. They are champions of "attachment parenting," the school of child-rearing that calls for a high level of closeness between parents and children. . . . Yet, their kids are, well, rude.*[43]

This is really a shame, because not only will we have to potentially deal with a generation of mannerless grown-ups in a decade, but also it's so much harder even in the short term on parents who have rude children. Raising socially well-behaved kids makes your life so much easier, and theirs, too. Our kid says thank you and please and excuse me, and every time he does he is showered with affection. The deli guy has a nickname for him. The firemen around the corner put him up in the truck. Babysitters want to come over. It requires constant vigilance and not getting him anything unless he asks politely, but wow, is it nice to not be ordered around by a three-foot-tall child.

Our Boomer parents encouraged us to question authority, and by and large made it clear that those in charge (including they themselves) weren't entirely reliable. But some old-fashioned things are there for a reason, and manners are one of them.

Other people's kids may be rude, but they can be avoided or ignored. Your kid you have to live with. When I got home, I thanked my lucky stars that I wasn't that mean kid's mother. No doubt she adores her child as much as I adore mine, and she should—especially because I don't know how anyone else could.

Share and Share Alike

One day, we were at the playground and came across this little wagon. My son, just a year old, started pushing it around a bit. From far away, echoing off the swings, we heard a scream: *"Noooooooon, bébé!"*

This French kid, probably age four or so, was losing it because a toddler was touching his toy. And his mother, rather than saying, "We're swinging now. You can let that baby look at your wagon," came over and took the wagon out of my son's hands and brought it to her son in the swing. He kept swinging, clutching his little wagon.

(Neal and I now use this around the house when we are anguished: *"Noooooooon, bébé!"*)

Now, I wasn't bothered by the child's behavior. Children often have trouble letting others share their things. What bothered me was the mother's reaction. Why do parents let their kids bring toys to the playground if they're not going to share them? This is one of my pet peeves. But what I find more annoying is that parents think their kids' feelings in those instances matter, and work so hard to cater to them.

Not to be blunt, but these are greedy toddlers! Who cares how they feel? What they want is immaterial to the situation. What matters is what they *do*.

This little girl brought an Elmo doll to the playground. My

son toddled up to her smiling. She clutched the doll as if he was a mugger and screamed at him rudely. I looked to her parents for some kind of "Now dear, you can't bring a toy to the playground if you're not going to share it;" or "Let's put that away if it's too special to you to share." Or even just a simple, "Don't scream at friendly children."

"She doesn't feel like sharing today," her mother said by way of explanation.

"So why did you come to the PLAYGROUND with a TOY?!" I felt like yelling. "I don't feel like wearing clothes, working, or being civil to you today, but I AM." And since when do toddlers "feel" like sharing? Never! They also don't "feel" like sleeping, eating, or doing lots of other things we make them do because we know better.

I see parents a bit too concerned with catering to "moods" and not giving kids this easy tool for getting past moods and getting on with the day. I am a firm believer in faking it till you make it when it comes to manners—I think behaving generously makes you internalize those values.

I love Miss Manners, and how Dr. Perri Klass summed her up in a 2009 article for the *New York Times* Science section: "I'm not telling you that you can't hate Tommy; I'm telling you that you can't hit Tommy. Your feelings are your own private business; your behavior is public."[44]

Kids have so many emotions. I think it is really good parenting to say they don't have to act on all of their emotions, and in fact that they can't act on all of them. It takes off the pressure and makes kids realize that all that fluctuation of mood and desire doesn't have to rule their life. And it reinforces the social contract that says we all have agreed to behave a certain way together (not hitting, not being mean, not being greedy), and that they can hold others to the same standard. Everyone benefits when everyone follows these basic rules of human decency.

Gen X parents are trying really hard to do a good job, and in the process sometimes making too big a deal out of a lot of things that should be simple. Like, there are times for eating and times for sleeping and times for TV and times for saying "Thank you" to the man at the store who gives you free gum.

You don't have to reinvent the protocol every day or every hour. It's the same day in and day out. You always say "Yes, please" when the fireman asks if you want to try on his helmet. You always say "Good morning" when the old lady on the stoop says "Hello."

Having good manners doesn't only make people like being around you more; it makes your life easier, because you know what to say in awkward situations. It makes kids more secure when they know the rules of polite society. Plus, thank-you cards yield more presents.

What I see happening a lot with our generation of parents is this desire to respect their children's unique sensibilities and moods. And it comes from a really good place. But we're going a bit far in the other direction and paying so much attention that we're picking up on every blip in our kids' whims. They want to sleep in Mommy and Daddy's bed! *Okay, we respect your feelings!* And Daddy sleeps on the floor! *Okay, we respect your feelings!*

How did it come to that? Does it really not matter what Mommy and Daddy want? Why ignore what you know instinctively is right for your household (Mommy and Daddy getting some time to themselves, for example)?

What's that saying, "Feelings aren't facts"? That's kind of handy. It's not denying your kids' feelings or disempowering them to insist that they share or say please. And sure, some days kids really *don't* feel like sharing. And on those days, they can do what we do as grown-ups when we need to take a break from polite society: stay home.

The Great Sleep-Training Debate

First, the good news: babies sleep a lot more than adults. Tons more. Say we need seven or eight hours. They need, like, fifteen. So getting eight hours a day is still totally doable. The problem is just that babies don't often sleep for very long stretches, so you have to get used to getting your sleep in little bursts.

For new parents, no topic is more charged than sleep: Why won't they sleep more? Why can't I ever sleep? And just how much sleep can a person do without until they can be declared legally dead?

Melissa Rayworth writes in an article called "The Sleepless Generation," "Babies who can't self-soothe quickly grow into preschoolers who won't sleep unless there's a cuddly parent in their bed. That leaves parents and kids exhausted, and marriages strained as couples either sleep separately or share their bed with one or more elbowing, teeth-grinding, frequently awakened offspring."[45]

Talking to experts on Generation X, Rayworth learned that our generation of parents is "putting their kids at risk in the name of protecting them from all discomfort."

And that is the number one reason you hear for why people don't let kids fall asleep by themselves: they cry, and crying must be stopped.

But I'm not so sure anymore that all crying is bad.

One of my friends has not slept more than three hours in a row since her son was born two years ago. We were at her son's second birthday party when she informed me that her lack of sleep was in fact entirely my fault.

Apparently, when our sons (born two weeks apart) were little babies, I had said, indignantly, "Can you believe people just leave their babies in the other room and let them cry until they fall asleep?! Even to the point where they puke!? Can you imagine what a monster you would have to be!?"

She was convinced by my tirade that sleep-training was evil. Cut to a few months later, when no one in my house was sleeping. I called my friend Tara and asked what to do and she said, "Dump him."

"What?" I said, horrified.

"Dump him," she repeated. "Put him in the crib. Let him fall asleep."

"But he's going to cry. A lot!"

"Yes, he is," she said. "The first night he may cry for an hour, the night after that for a half hour, and the night after that for a few minutes. But the rest of your lives, he will be able to fall asleep by himself and when he wakes up at night he will be able to put himself back to sleep and you'll all get more sleep and save tons of tears in the long run."

I wasn't sure I could stomach it, so I turned to the parenting sections of various bookstores. No books helped, but some helped less than others. Anything that advised me to hug it out or give it time only made me angry. I didn't want to pretend we weren't in the midst of a sleep emergency, and I didn't want a guilt trip for wanting to help my child (and myself) get to sleep. I instinctively knew we had to do something. I just wasn't sure what.

My nemesis during this time? Elizabeth Pantley, the parenting expert who appears in one of her promo pictures sitting on a bed with her husband and their four children. All are wearing matching blue-and-white cloud pajamas and smiling beatifically.

When I was trying to get Oliver to fall asleep on his own, the last book in the world I needed to read was Pantley's *The No Cry Sleep Solution*. I was feeling wishy-washy and eager to put off letting him cry. I was anxious and depressed by the prospect of having to admit we had a problem. So when I read that book and it told me I was right to not want to hear him cry, that I should just journal the problem, and make lots of charts about his sleep patterns and try to gently nudge and . . .

I tried to convince my husband that we should go this route and he just stared at me and said, "Do you actually think that's going to work?"

I had to admit that I did not, that the book did not even guarantee that it would "work" in the way we wanted a sleep plan to work—that is, to result in lots more sleep for everyone.

What I needed was some hardcore advice to balance out my natural sappiness. You don't need books that fit in with your "philosophy." You need books that balance out your instincts, show you the other side. Everyone needs a devil's advocate so they don't become wedded to an extreme position.

My friend who never cleans her house, who is totally over-whelmed and exhausted, I encourage to get more childcare, to plan out her days more rigorously, to go to a Container Store already. My friend who is super-meticulous and almost Step-ford Wife–ish I tell to loosen up on the gourmet meals already, work more on her own moneymaking projects, and let the house go to hell once in a while.

Finally, we asked Oliver's pediatrician what to do. When Oliver was eight months old and still waking up and calling for us a couple of times a night, we asked his doctor if we should try sleep-training.

"Dr. Ferber isn't really popular right now," he admitted, "but he was right about some things. You really do need to let babies learn how to fall asleep on their own."

"So, we've either walked or nursed him to sleep most nights. When should we start letting him fall asleep on his own?"

Our doctor smiled compassionately and said: "Yesterday."

As vehement as the "No Cry" books and online message boards were about how "abandoning" your baby to cry would damage her for life, our friends were equally adamant that this was by far the lesser of parenting evils.

"Sleep-training Myha was the hardest thing I ever did, but also the best," our friend Logan said. He did a slower version where, instead of "dumping," he and his wife went in and reas-sured his daughter at certain intervals. It took them a week, at the end of which for nighttime and naps, he would lay her down, and she would wave "bye-bye" and roll over and fall asleep.

We decided to go with Tara and the quick-like-a-Band-Aid hardcore route. That night we did our whole nighttime routine, but instead of letting him fall asleep being rocked or nursed, we put him down sleepy.

He was perplexed at first, then furious. He screamed for twenty minutes solid.

I went in and explained to him that he had to go to sleep and that we were there if he needed anything but he just needed to fall asleep now. This stoked his rage. I retreated back to our room, where Neal and I sat on the bed and stared at each other miserably.

I felt like the worst person who had ever lived. I yelled at Neal that he was making me torture our child. We both almost went in and got him every thirty seconds, but held each other back. And then . . . he fell asleep. He woke up a couple more times and we let him fall back asleep on his own, hard as it was not to go in there. Each bout lasted only a few minutes, but it felt like hours. By the next morning I was determined to see this through, but also convinced it was a terrible, futile process that would only make the child hate us and cause him to never sleep again out of spite.

The next night we did the same thing and again he was furious, but the crying was not as fierce and lasted only half as long, and he quieted right back when he woke up in the middle of the night.

On day three, he just went quietly to sleep and slept twelve hours straight.

The biggest surprise: throughout these three days of trial, he didn't seem scarred. He didn't even seem to hold it against us. He woke up happy and stayed happy all day. What happened to the neuroses that this parenting method was supposed to cause? To the sense of abandonment and horror we would encounter? I didn't see it. He just seemed better rested than he ever had been. He had an extra spring in his step—crawl, rather. I certainly felt brighter. I was getting eight hours of sleep a night for the first time since the second trimester of pregnancy.

Anyway, my friend Ondine stood there while we watched our sons splash around in the kiddie pool and told me she wished I had told her I'd had such a change of heart. "He's two! Now it's too late!" she wailed.

I called Tara. She said, "It's never too late. I imagine it's just a little harder if they're big enough to get out of their crib and try to break down your door."

Try typing something like that into a parenting message board and see what happens. Few things get other parents more riled up than "cry it out" sleep-training. One of the many horrible things the anti camp says will happen is that you will become "desensitized" to your child's cries.

First of all: you don't.

Second of all: isn't that a shame! Why should it be a negative to become desensitized? It seems good to get to the point where you don't completely freak out when your kid cries. I wish I didn't have that crazy, primal, *the sabertooths are coming* alarm go off when he cries. I have gotten to the point where I can apply a Band-Aid to a scooter injury with a steady hand, but inside my head part of me is screaming, "That's it! That's it! I am a terrible mother to have let him get this ghastly wound! I must never let him ride that horrid thing again!"

And then, of course, he's back off scooting and I'm back to my conversations with other parents moments after the emotional storm.

In closing, one thing I can say anecdotally is that sleep-training tends to be really healthy for relationships. Few are the families who aren't stressed out by a baby who can't fall asleep on his own. If it takes listening to your baby cry for a couple of nights while he learns to self-soothe to buy your family years of bedtime peace, and a few adults-only hours of the night, that seems like an okay deal.

Anxiety-Free Potty-Training

"Don't freak out" is a friend's sole advice about potty-training. She says it doesn't matter whether you do it at age two or three, by degrees or all at once, with or without Pull-Ups. Just don't freak out and you're golden, she says. But freak out, turn on the pressure, or set timetables, and look out.

I haven't freaked out. I also haven't done it. But I figure we'll get to it this summer, when we can go up to the country and Oliver can run around naked. In Sweden, every kid around the age of three is potty-trained during the six-week vacation everyone in the country takes in July. That seems pretty efficient.

There's a whole market around potty-training, from the *Elmo's Potty Time* DVD to *The Potty Book* to a million other books, movies, special potties, and now even potty-training "Booty Camp." It doesn't seem like there's anything wrong with indulging kids' fascination with the process, but it also doesn't seem remotely necessary.

Maybe I'm becoming a broken record, but I really don't understand why people are making parenting so complex. The best example of this trend toward complication I've seen so far is "Elimination Communication," whereby parents forgo diapers altogether and hang their baby over a toilet from a young age, making a cue noise like "sssssssssssssssss" to get them to pee. When it comes to their babies' pooping, parents look for signs that they're ready to go and then hang them over the toilet the same way.

Wow, does this seem like a lot of work! First of all, you have to be by a bathroom at all times, and if you leave your baby with anyone else for any amount of time, the other person has to be trained to make noises like "sssssssssssssssss" and to keep their eyes on the baby for signs of an impending bowel movement. Give me diapers anytime.

The truth is, having a potty-trained kid is not so unlike having a non-potty-trained kid. Where the kid goes is just a detail. And like everything else, it's a trade-off. Diapers provide convenience. You don't have to stop the car five times in an hour so you can let a kid out of her car seat to pee. Potty-training provides less intimate contact with one's child's waste. Of course eventually the kid has to do it so he can go to kindergarten and various other places for which you need to be potty-trained. But what's the rush? This is one of a great number of situations where there's a perfectly sizeable window of time within which you're fine if you do, fine if you don't.

Postpartum and
Postpostpartum Depression

Maternity leave was a revelation. Suddenly, for a few weeks, all I had to do was love my baby. I was still getting paid, even! Plus, thanks to a C-section, I was on Percocet for the first couple of weeks, which let me float around the city on a double high of hormones and painkillers.

With a relatively easy, happy baby and a supportive, at-home husband, I spent those first days enjoying the city. I was breastfeeding and it was summer, so we didn't have to pack more than a few diapers in my purse. Neal and I went to museums. We went on picnics. We would get iced coffees and muffins and sit in the park, staring in wonder at the tiny creature in the sling. When he got hungry, I nursed him. Mostly, as we wandered around, he slept against my body.

Even our social life didn't disappear. We went to dinner parties. We had people over for wine and take-out pizza.

I was the opposite of depressed . . . until Oliver was a few months and I started getting incredibly irritable and weepy. In retrospect it may have had something to do with the hormone changes around starting to wean.

But whatever the reason, it sucked. At all times, a dull roar of depletion, sadness, and anger echoed around in my head, making me distracted and distant. The smallest thing would make me burst into tears. I snapped at any perceived criticism. I was paranoid and resentful and felt a lot like I was going crazy. When I started crying, which was typically once a day, I couldn't stop until I was totally exhausted. Neal was concerned, but also baffled and didn't know what to do other than go along with my diagnosis of "panic attacks caused by too much work."

I was working full-time as an editor, half the week at home, plus doing two part-time writing jobs at night after Oliver went to bed. There wasn't a second of free time in my schedule. If I took even thirty minutes away from either work or Oliver to watch a sitcom, I felt guilty. So it was a pretty reasonable guess that overwork was the reason for my anxiety.

But when I went into a shrink's office to see if he could advise me on how to get over my panic attacks, he asked me to describe them. Then he said, "There's no crying in panic attacks. You have clinical depression. I'm going to write you a prescription."

I laughed at his inadvertent reference to *A League of Their Own*: "There's no crying in baseball," which I had often said to myself in an attempt to get it together.

And then I fought his diagnosis. I explained how that was impossible. I was so high functioning! Could someone who was clinically depressed handle three jobs and a baby? I didn't think so. And I came from a family with lots of alcoholics and depressives in it but I didn't drink much at all, at least not since my twenties, and I was usually very chipper.

But I undermined my argument, because in the course of my filibuster I burst into tears.

"So many people I know are on medication!" I said between sobs. "I'm the one who can keep it together without antidepressants. I'm the sane one! I don't need drugs!"

"Does depression run in your family?" the doctor asked calmly.

"Yes," I muttered. I took the scrip.

I started taking the low-dose pills, walking to work rather than taking the subway, and seeing a therapist once a week. Within a month, I felt like every cliché in every Zoloft ad: like the clouds had lifted, like a weight had left my shoulders, like myself again. I wasn't crying all the time. I enjoyed playing with toy trains about a million percent more. Being in therapy helped me learn how to say no to extra work, to make time for movies and my friends and just sitting around at the playground doing nothing but watching Oliver run around.

I'd like to think I was a fine mother while I was depressed, that I covered well, that I passed. But I'm sure Oliver would have noticed eventually that in my miserable state I wasn't totally present, if he hadn't already. Staying unhappy wouldn't have been fair to him, let alone to me or to Neal.

I owed it to everyone to face up to how unhappy I was, and to do something about it. Tom Cruise may yammer on about aliens and exercise, and he may believe antidepressants are some kind of great delusion. But to me, they made a world of difference. I admitted needing help so that I could be happier and therefore a better parent and spouse and person. I got help, and lo, I was no longer yelling at people who bumped into me on the sidewalk or zoning out during sing-alongs. There's certainly no shame in doing what needs to be done to be there for your family, and for you.

Sex and Marriage

I have a secret. I still have sex with my husband. And . . . shhhh . . . more than once a month. More, even, than once a week. But around most parents I can't talk about it, for fear of seeming boastful or rude. Meanwhile, people are constantly talking about how they're never having sex since the baby came—or, more often, joking about it in a bitter way. Just try to admit to a sex life when you're in the middle of a circle of people saying, "I'd so much rather sleep than have sex." Sure, sometimes. But *every night*?

A coworker and I recently "came out" to each other as parents who still have sex. In the urge to normalize libidoless marriages, self-help books and mainstream magazines have made it seem weird to *not* have sex problems postbaby. What's followed is a kind of bragging: "Oh, I never have sex with my partner" has joined the "I never sleep / take a shower / go to the movies" chorus of complaints that are designed to bond new parents to one another and make people who are unhappy feel like they're *supposed* to feel that way.

But what if you still make time to have sex in those three hours after the baby goes to sleep but before you do? What if you taught your baby to self-soothe and now he doesn't wake up four times a night just to be held and lulled back to sleep? What if you take a shower in the half hour that the kid watches *Sesame Street* and eats Cheerios in the morning? What if you plunk down the $40 and get a babysitter once a month so you can go see a blockbuster and get your fix of fake-buttered popcorn?

You're left out of the circle of moaning, that's what. Of course, you also are clean, rested, relaxed, and up on the latest action movies, which is, believe it or not, plenty of consolation.

I hate whining. Doing it pretty much never makes me feel better. And listening to it drives me crazy. I'd much rather get mad or cry and then figure out a solution or get in a fight. That's productive. Whining—and especially whining with others—just maintains a disappointing status quo.

And it really seems like a self-fulfilling prophecy so much of the time. People who dread being pregnant and anticipate discomfort tend to have a harder time of it.

Of course it's not like you want to go into things with superhigh expectations or unrealistic ambitions about how easy everything's going to be. There is a recent documentary called *Orgasmic Birth* that is the ultimate example of setting the bar a bit too high. But you also don't want to curse yourself or pretend it's normal to give up on sex, movies, showers, and the rest of it. Everything is different when you become a parent, but that doesn't mean anything is *impossible*.

It just becomes about trade-offs. During the baby's nap, do you mop the floor, sleep with your spouse, do an hour of work, cook a lasagna, take a shower, take a nap yourself, call a friend, read the paper, watch TV? Lots of options. You just have to figure out your priorities. I don't mind grubby floors or take-out, so I usually opt for taking a shower and then reading the paper while watching TV and/or sex, but if you wanted a home-cooked meal and a clean floor, you could pass up the news that day.

To get back on topic: failing to ever make sex a priority—opting instead always for TV or mopping the floor—is really dangerous for a relationship. Not only is sex a fun thing, it's a big part of what binds couples together. And bonding with each other is really important. It's really easy to let hanging out with your partner slip to the bottom of a very long to-do list. But other things can wait. When the kids are sleeping, we need to remember to enjoy all the perks that go along with being grown-ups.

Language Development Craziness

A major source of parenting freak-outs around the second year is a child's lack of verbal ability. Some children start talking early, others late. Sometimes talking late is a sign of something like autism or a learning disability. Plenty of times it's not. But there's always an article around to stoke the anxiety regarding this issue.

In a March 1, 2009, op-ed for the *New York Times* called "One Ride Forward, Two Steps Back," M. Suzanne Zeedyk, a senior lecturer in developmental psychology at the University of Dundee, wrote, "Are forward-facing strollers having a negative effect on babies' language development? British teachers have for some time been observing a decline in the linguistic abilities of many children, and some have wondered whether this might be one contributing factor."[46]

The author doesn't offer any substantial evidence. Her most scientific move was watching 2,700 people strolling with their children and noting: "When traveling with their babies in forward-facing strollers, caregivers were observed speaking to infants in only eleven percent of cases, while the figure was twenty-five percent for those using toward-facing strollers, and even higher for those carrying children or walking with them."

The op-ed closes with a call for stroller designers to look into producing affordable strollers that face both ways. The author says the study wasn't meant to solve anything, just to raise questions.

I have some questions.

What percentage of a child's well-being really has to do with which way her stroller faces rather than, say, whether or not she has enough food to eat, enough sleep, enough love? Like .00009 percent? And so does this issue really seem like the best allocation of our op-ed pages and child-wares industry?

Or, to quote a comedian: "CANCER, YOU PEOPLE! WE STILL DON'T HAVE A CURE FOR CANCER!"

Also: Do people really need to be told to talk to their children? And do people really need to talk to their children twenty-four hours a day? Isn't there something to be said for living in the present? For silently enjoying a moment together? I don't know about you, but I think it's totally educational to watch people and trees and cars go by without incessantly asking Junior, "What *color* is that car? Do you see a *circle*? *How many* pigeons are there on that mailbox? Good job!"

Is every stroller outing about pushing along our children's language development rather than, say, showing them the world, lulling them to sleep, or, I don't know, getting from your house to the grocery store and back?

And I know this is just bitchy, but I feel like given the subjectivity of this writer's anecdotal research, mine is just as valid: here in New York, of the 2,700-plus people I've seen walking around with their kids in the last couple of weeks, the only ones I've seen with the backward-facing strollers are bored nannies pushing zoned-out babies.

And if my hilariously chatty kid has been linguistically delayed by being in a forward-facing stroller, I shudder to think how much he'd be talking if he'd been facing me instead.

The Almighty Nap

Oliver and I had a great time at the playground. But the whole time I was thinking, *I can't wait for his nap so I can get some work done.* The house needed straightening. I would do that, then finish reading Ann Hulbert's *Raising America*, write a chapter of my book, and then take a twenty-minute nap. If Oliver slept a long time, I could even call my friend Tara and catch up with her.

I cooed at Oliver, who was clearly tired, through lunch. I changed his diaper, got him all cozy, and tucked him into his bed. "I don't want to take a nap!" he yelled. I insisted he needed one. We had a birthday party to go to when he woke up. He was tired. It was naptime.

He screamed, but I closed the door.

And at this moment, he learned how to climb out of his crib, which he proceeded to do twenty times in a row. I put him back each time and with increasing agitation told him to go to sleep.

Finally, he ran out of his room and into mine, and crawled into bed. "Sleep in Mama-Dada's bed!" he proclaimed.

"And you'll sleep?" I asked. He said he would, and snuggled under the covers.

Okay, I thought, *I'll just do the nap first.* I was pretty exhausted. So I cuddled up next to him and immediately started to drift off. Thirty seconds later, I opened my eyes and saw Oliver had turned the bedside light on and was about to jump on my head from the bedside table.

What, fellow parents, is the right thing to do in such a scenario?

Here's what I did: I gave up on him taking a nap, put on a Disney film, and slept next to him for twenty minutes while he watched the movie. At the end of this time, I switched off the TV and played with him for an hour (mostly chase games, but also hide-and-seek, tea party, horsey, and a game referred to informally as Monster coming! Run!).

I did the dishes while he played with trucks. I called Tara and in spite of a few interruptions ("Mama! I need a diaper!") managed to get in a good ten-minute chat. And he got to talk to his godmother, too. "Whatchoo doing, Tara?" (Pause.) "I'm a *leeeetle* boy!" (Pause) "Bye!"

We went to the party and then to a playdate at his best friend's house. He got totally exhausted and went to bed an hour earlier than usual, leaving me free to finish Hulbert's book and write a chapter (hi there). So everything I'd wanted to do eventually got done. My agitation wasn't necessary, and I really had to just let it go and change tacks.

I realize now that I was hinging too much on the nap. I'd become dependent on it, and romanticized that time too much. The truth is, if he'd napped, I probably would have watched a half hour of CNN, read two pages, and then slept for an hour. That wasn't the only time span at our disposal. The day is long, and the night is even longer.

Danger!

When I gave Oliver one of his first baths, his head slipped under the water for a second. I was convinced I'd drowned him. My proof that he was near death even though he still had his eyes open and appeared to be breathing? *He didn't cry! Why wasn't he crying?!* He'd been *underwater*!

It took me many minutes of staring at him wrapped up in that towel blinking to convince myself that not only did he probably not have brain damage but also he'd barely even noticed what looked to me like a brush with death.

I realized in that moment how vulnerable babies seem and how responsible one is for their continued existence. It made me better understand a helicopter mother whose toddler I used to babysit. She would scream if I walked her son under a ceiling fan, even if it was switched off. "It could fall on his head!" she would squeal.

"And a car could crash through the side of the building," I wanted to say. "But we can't anticipate every single threat, can we?"

She thought we could. Or she was going to try, by God. That little boy practically had to wear a helmet whenever he left his room.

It's hard to know what to really worry about these days, because there are warnings about almost every conceivable product, food, and activity, and they change constantly. You are not supposed to eat fish when you're pregnant because of the mercury—but you are supposed to eat it because of the omega-3. You aren't supposed to give a baby a plastic bottle because it might leach BPA—but you're not supposed to use glass because it could break and cut the baby. You're not supposed to use a pacifier because it could cause "nipple confusion," but pacifiers supposedly diminish the risk for SIDS (aka crib death), which sounds a bit more terrifying than your baby mixing up flesh and silicone.

The CDC has this awesome series called "Protect the Ones You Love" with practical, fact-based advice about limiting hazards.[47] Each starts out with this little pep talk: "We all want to keep our children safe and secure and help them live to their full potential. Knowing how to prevent leading causes of child injury, like road traffic injuries, is a step toward this goal."

When it comes to nonfatal injuries, the CDC reports that: "Falls are the leading cause of nonfatal injuries for all children ages zero to nineteen. Every day, approximately 8,000 children are treated in U.S. emergency rooms for fall-related injuries. This adds up to almost 2.8 million children each year."

The fear-generating issues you hear about so much these days—Bisphenol-A in baby bottles, "toxic mattresses," off-gassing, lead paint on toys—are microscopically small threats by comparison.

Lenore Skenazy, author of Wiley's 2009 book *Free-Range Kids: Giving Our Kids the Freedom We Had Without Going Nuts with Worry,* argues that it's a mistake to keep such close reins on our kids. She says we had a ton of freedom as kids, and we should extend that same freedom to our children. Skenazy writes

Any kid killed is a horrible tragedy. It makes my stomach plunge to even think about it. But when the numbers are about 50 kids in a country of 300 million, it's also a very random, rare event. It is far more rare, for instance, than dying from a fall off the bed or other furniture. So should we, for safety's sake, all start sleeping on the floor?

I'm with her. And yet, I wonder if we're so eager to over-protect our kids because we had too much freedom as children. We're not so sure there are any more dangers lurking out there than ever before, but we are sure that there are times we wished we had more attention, and so we're going to make sure our own children never want for a sense of security.

There should be better product testing, yes. It is true that lots of stuff from China has lately been found to be dangerous. And when kids put lead-painted toys in their mouths, they are in fact possibly affecting their lead levels. And it is true that that stuff doesn't last long. On a trip to Greece, we bought a Greek toy and a Chinese toy from the same store. Initially, the Chinese toy (a mouse with a bell attached to a stick that rang when you pushed it) and the Greek toy (a grasshopper pull-toy) seemed to be about the same level of craftsmanship. The Greek toy just was about twice as expensive. But the Greek toy continues to be a fun thing to pull around and looks the same as it did the day we got it, whereas the Chinese toy lasted about two weeks and then imploded in a shower of splinters.

I guess there's no harm in monitoring obscure potential dangers if that's what you're into, but there are plenty of real threats and basic things to do about them (bars on windows, bleach on a high shelf, car seats). It may be that some hysterical blog warning against, like, fleece pajamas, has it right, and lamb jammies are going to kill off a generation, but I choose to believe that what everyone else is doing is reasonably okay, enough okay that most of them will make it to adulthood with no more than a few scars and only a few alarming stories to tell.

School Days

An acquaintance of mine recently told me about his ordeal applying to pre-kindergartens in New York City. For one school, the four-year-old was subjected to a battery of tests, plus an interview, alone, with a school official. The child reported being asked common-knowledge questions like, "What is a babysitter for?" But of course he could give his parents no indication of how well he did. They would just have to wait for the scores to roll in. The testing, by the way, cost $500. If they got into the school, it would be $30,000 a year. That's a hell of a lot of crayons.

And a hell of a lot of pressure.

What if the kid was having a bad day come test time? What if he was tired, hadn't eaten enough, or was cranky? What if he was in one of those developmental stages where he needed to sleep more to gear up for some new jump in language acquisition? What if he was sad his goldfish had just died? What if he didn't like the testers?

It didn't matter. He was expected to suck it up, put on his four-year-old game face, and give it his best shot. The ability to deliver, to show up at go-time, all cylinders pumping, is something even pro athletes can't always do. After thirty-two years, I've learned how to keep myself from crying at the office, how to pretend I'm having a good time at a party where I'm miserable, and how to get myself out of the house, get the kid to school, and go to work even on days when I feel rotten. But to expect this of anyone under the age of thirty, let alone under the age of five, seems pretty harsh.

But preschool can make otherwise sane parents crazy.

"I work so much that I need school to be a surrogate parent," I overheard a parent who'd gotten her daughter into a famous and high-quality private school saying. "Now I know she's set through high school. I don't have to worry about her anymore." I think she probably meant she didn't have to worry about the school hunt anymore, but the slip was telling: she could just leave all the headaches of child-rearing in the capable hands of those teachers and administrators to whom she was paying tens of thousands of dollars a year.

Oliver goes to a lovely little grassroots nonprofit school near our apartment. We picked it because we saw the teachers with the kids on the local playground and they all seemed really nice and happy. Also, there was a one-page application that asked for the child's name and birthday and the parent's name (other parent optional). That was it. No ERB testing. No interviews; just first-come, first-serve. It was just a few hours a week. The kids spend a lot of time at the playground, and then playing with Play-Doh, painting, and doing whatever activities they want within the sweetly arranged classroom.

It seemed totally bucolic. In fact, everyone loved it so much that the school was overrun with people who wanted to stay there and so the upper classes predictably couldn't give all families their first choice for schedules. This led, rather shockingly I thought, to a revolt. Irate parents sent mass e-mails around asking for—nay, demanding!—meetings with the director, who'd gone out of her way to work out a solution that allowed everyone already at the school to stay, if at different hours than they'd originally chosen.

It was so weird to me what a couple of the parents in particular complained about. First of all, they insisted that the school's director *did not understand* their concerns. *She must be made to understand how upset we are!* they concurred.

Why? I wondered. I mean, I was quite sure she did understand. She was being barraged with e-mails, after all. But what did it matter whether she did or not if there was nothing else she could do? Reshuffling classes was the only workable solution besides randomly expelling kids.

The other thing some parents got mad about was the prospect that their young-three-year-olds would be with old-two-year-olds. "The curriculum won't be challenging enough!" one of the mothers exclaimed. We are talking about children who have only been walking for a couple of years. Seems like there's lots of time for challenging curriculums.

A teacher I know tells me about one family convinced their child is "gifted and talented." No matter that there's no evidence of this; the parents are convinced, and so they've worked hard to bully the teachers and principal into giving her special status—a class apart from her peers. The teachers have offered extra work, more advanced books, a million other things, but the parents don't want any of that. They want to have a "gifted" child in a "gifted" program; never mind that at this public school there is no such thing, and that if there were, their daughter would likely not qualify for it.

Sandra Tsing Loh's book *Mother on Fire* describes the intense school application process, and the parental insecurities it plays upon. She recalls the tours of elite private schools and how frenzied the parents were to get their child in. Then one day she wanders over to her local, almost all-Hispanic public school and takes a tour. She sees dedicated teachers and a devoted principal. She immediately signs up her kid, the only blond child for miles, and they discover she gets a great education. None of the fears the elite schools prey upon ever materialize.

When it comes to my son's nursery school, the parents who demanded a challenge seemed off base. These are kids who aren't totally potty-trained and can't tie their shoes; *everything* is challenging for them. The school focuses on the kids' relationships. They play all day and treat one another well. When I see them run into each other on the playground, they greet each other sweetly and hug. They'll have lots of time to learn their letters and numbers, to do colors and shapes. But learning how to make and keep friends is more valuable than all those things, and I'm glad it's the first skill these young children are being taught.

Becoming Like
Our Parents—or Not

In a March 2009 article in the *New York Times* called "When Grandma Can't Be Bothered," Joanne Kaufman writes that many Baby Boomers are far too busy with their own lives to care for their grandchildren.[48] She quotes Dr. Gail Saltz, a Manhattan psychiatrist, as saying, "This generation [Generation X] does the helicopter parenting so they're omni-available, omnipresent and omni-facilitating compared to the previous generation. I often hear from grandparents that their children are overindulgent with time and attention."

It makes sense that the Baby Boomers are so often wringing their hands about their children's indulgent parenting. It goes so against the grain of the demographic's own child-rearing philosophy—which started with Dr. Spock's "You know more than you think you do" and ended with a kind of distracted, laissez-faire approach.

Hilariously, Boomers do appear to have some concerns about their role as grandparents. Namely, they want to make sure their name doesn't make them sound old.

The *Wall Street Journal's* 2009 article "A Grandma or Grandpa by Any Other Name Is Just as Old" noted that grandparents today are struggling with a lot of issues: "How to be attentive grandparents while having a busy career and, increasingly, caring for their own elderly parents? How to stay close to the tykes while living far away? But one of the most vexing issues they face is deciding what they want to be called by their grandchildren, lest it make them sound—and feel—old."[49] They're coming up with plenty of alternative and younger-sounding names for themselves—like "Glamma."

Baby Boomers don't make the best lot of grandparents in the world. But then again, no generation of grandparents has ever been perfect, or appropriately appreciated. As Ann Hulbert wrote in her great survey of American parenting history, at the science-minded turn of the twentieth century, "Victorian ministers and their grandmotherly allies had been dismissed as the outmoded voice of soft dogma and 'uncertain instinct.'"[50]

My parents are devoted to their grandson. They adore him. He adores them. It is so sweet to see them together. And they've been terrific for much of the last three years. When Neal's left town, my mother has come over daily to help me. My father has given his grandson countless tractor rides and baths.

And yet, having a baby has made me more aware of their limits. My mother had promised herself as a "full-time grandmother," but the week I was to return to work from maternity leave, she said she didn't think she'd be able to do so much after all. She was too busy with her own life, and too "old and tired." (My mother is in her midsixties, looks fifty, and has been known to carry dressers up stairs by herself, so this didn't entirely fly as an excuse.) She just wasn't up to it.

Looking back, it was expecting too much to see her as our

sole childcare salvation. She's awfully busy and we shouldn't have let her sign on for so much in the first place. So Neal did most of the work-hours childcare for the first year and then I got a raise and we were able to afford a babysitter for ten hours a week so he could get a break.

My mother never gave me advice about breastfeeding, even though she'd done it. I'm sure she would have, but I never even asked. She did say that when she started, she was watching the clock and doing ten minutes on each boob and was relieved when someone finally told her she didn't have to do that. But I think I actually sent her out of the room when the lactation-consultant nurses came in the day Oliver was born. My mother did encourage me to do cry-it-out sleep-training, but I didn't do that until I'd been told the same thing by two friends I trusted plus our pediatrician.

Our relationship with our own parents plays such a role in how we raise our kids, whether we're copying them or trying not to. We recapitulate our own relations with our mothers, and when we see them around our kids, it can make us crazy, or make us cut them more slack, depending.

One friend of mine said, "My mother was crazy so I am always trying to prove that I'm not crazy." Her mother was also overweight, so it's not surprising that you've never seen a skinnier, in-better-shape person than my friend, who runs miles a day and never seems to eat more than the occasional piece of fruit.

Sometimes having a baby makes people way closer to their parents. ("I have so much more respect for them now!") Sometimes having a baby makes people way more critical of their parents. ("I can't believe they didn't do XYZ!")

My parents were always complimenting me as a child for

being so independent and "such a trouper." A lot of the stories they tell revolve around me showing dazzling precocity and unfailing self-knowledge, even as a toddler.

"You told us you wouldn't like Disneyland until you were five, and you were right!"

"When you were two, we went on a long walk through the Texas desert in the blazing summer sun, and you didn't complain once! I realized at the end that we probably should have carried you. . . . Such a trouper!"

Needless to say, Oliver gets carried a lot, and cuddled a lot, and probably coddled a bit too much sometimes.

One woman I know who was abused as a child has become supermom. She was hell-bent on breaking the cycle, and she has. Her children are devoted to her. She is loving and sweet and generous with them. She has provided a wonderful house, a doting father, and unconditional love. How she managed to do all this when she had no firsthand experience of such good parenting is a mystery to me. And it suggests to me that we really do have an instinct for this.

"We're born with the instinct for parenting," one pediatrician told me, "but the expression of that instinct is learned. We can be taught how to apply our instincts. That's why abused children so often abuse their own children. That's how they learned to express their parenting instincts."

Another friend and his sister had a kind of awful childhood and so they just never had children of their own. They never liked being children, and in their experience it had only made their own parents miserable, so they opted out.

If your parents don't pay enough attention to your child, or if they try to take over, or if they make any of a million different kinds of missteps, it can damage your relationship with them and call up your own insecurities and grudges from childhood.

Then again, if they are good and kind with your child and helpful to you in a crunch, it can forgive a world of hurt from your own childhood.

Neal was out of town for a week recently and my mother was there every day. Now that Oliver's two and a half, he's not quite as exhausting as when he was a baby so it's easier for people to watch him. And he and my mom really enjoy each other. When I come home from work and find them playing Legos on the floor or watching *Cinderella*, I think how lucky I am, and how lucky Oliver is, to have Granny and Poppa in his life.

First Friendships

One of my favorite new phases in the past year has been Oliver's development of really good friends. He has a tendency to say, to anyone he's enjoying at that moment, "You're my best friend!" He says it to his grandmother, to me, to some random kid who happens to be sharing nicely in the truck pit on the playground, or to the charismatic older girl at the playground whom my mother continually reminds me bears an unfortunate resemblance to Patty McCormick, the child actress who portrayed a killer in *The Bad Seed*.

But the funniest thing about it is that he actually has best friends.

Oliver's teacher told me Aims and another boy at school got in an argument one day about who was Oliver's best friend. "We tried to tell them they were both Oliver's friends," the teacher said, sweetly.

"Well, that was very nice of you," I said, "but next time, you can break up the fight by telling that other boy Oliver's never even mentioned him, and that Aims has long been, and most definitely still is, Oliver's best friend."

The teacher laughed and said she'd try that. (I knew she wouldn't, but it was a funny mental image: this saintly preschool teacher quietly breaking it to a little boy that she had it on good authority that he was not, in fact, the BFF of another kid.)

Oliver asks for his closest friends when he hasn't seen them in a while. Sometimes he is more in the mood for one or the other and will request them. "I want to go to Aims's house!" or "I want to go to the park with Ella!" For other kids he has less passionate but periodically intense affections.

It's so exciting when kids make friends, especially really nice friends. Watching them interact on the playground and fall for each other is one of the sweetest things I can imagine. They brighten up when the other walks into the playground. They hug and kiss and walk around holding hands. Ella and Oliver insist on hiding in the closet together and jumping on the bed. When they're at our place they scurry over the bed and onto the long bedside table, then push the clock radio on. They sway to whatever Beyoncé song is on and giggle together.

I hope he always has this: these friends he enjoys, who enjoy him, who he has funny little rituals with, who make him light up when they arrive at the door, who invite him to play in the dirt with trucks or to run through the sprinklers holding hands. I don't know that early childhood friendships have any staying power, or signify any future success in socializing or romance, but when kids care about each other even as they are in toddler turmoil, it can't be a bad sign, right?

Cracking the Whip

"Children without bedtimes seem pale and anxious," a friend of mine says, and I think she's right. Little kids without rules get kind of twitchy and insecure. It is just our projection that makes us think they want freedom of choice—just like we project a need for variety onto cats and get them twelve different kinds of Fancy Feast. They'd be perfectly happy with Gourmet Chicken every morning and night.

Kids do benefit from a varied food diet, but not so much from a varied set of rules. It makes them feel unstable. Selma H. Fraiberg's *The Magic Years: Understanding and Handling the Problems of Early Childhood* explains how a little kid's mind works:

> *He discovers that if he turns the knob on the television set certain pictures appear. He repeats the experiment several hundred times so we cannot suspect him of drawing inferences from an inadequate number of trials and we can't speak a word against the statistical method employed here. On the basis of this perfectly valid research procedure he is able to conclude and confirm each time that it is he who makes the little people come out of the box by turning the switch!*[51]

In other words, if they open an off-limits kitchen drawer again and again, it's not "testing" in the way it's often used.

They're not trying to make you crazy or test your nerves. They're testing to make sure the rule is still the same, because if the rule is the same, then all is not chaos.

"Am I still not allowed to open this drawer?" they are asking with their actions. "Yes, this drawer is still off limits," they say to themselves, relieved, when you scold them for getting into it. "Is it still off limits?" they wonder again ten minutes later.

My friend Ondine found this period remarkably easy. "Why are they called the terrible twos?" she wondered. "They're terrific!"

She'd had such a hard time with her son's babyhood: he never slept, he barely ate, and he needed a surgery. Now he plays by himself for stretches of time and can tell her what he needs. She has so much fun with him now. And she doesn't even mind the tantrums. "He gets really mad sometimes," she says shrugging. "So? So do I."

One day when I picked up Oliver from school, he told me he'd gotten in trouble. I was surprised, as his teachers hadn't mentioned it and they usually do if a kid has misbehaved. "What did you do?" I asked.

"I pushed Dylan E.," he said, rather giddily.

"Really?" I asked. I don't know why, but I didn't quite believe him. Maybe it was because when he gets in trouble he usually freaks out completely (he's his mother's son), and he was totally not freaked out. He seemed thrilled.

"Yes! And I got a time-out! And I sat on the bench! And I cried!"

When I asked his teacher the next school day, she was stumped. "No, he's never done anything like that," she said. "He and Dylan play kind of rough sometimes, but . . . nope."

But then, the next week, he totally did get in trouble! He tried to kick Dylan E. in the head when they were struggling at the top of a slide. He missed, but nevertheless was punished for his intention, and had a time-out on the bench with one of the teachers.

His teacher told me when I picked him up. She mentioned the foreshadowing the week before. "He must be psychic," the teacher said, rather amused.

I asked Oliver about it on the way home. He described the incident without the same enthusiasm, but with evident satisfaction. He had been curious about what getting in trouble at school was like. Now he knew. He didn't like it, necessarily, but he seemed glad to know what the story was.

We had serious conversations about not hurting friends, but I knew he knew all that. And I didn't blame him for testing the system in this way, especially because no one actually got hurt. I was such a goody two-shoes I remember being terrified of getting in trouble. Maybe if I'd just gotten in trouble once early on, I could have gotten over that phobia once and for all.

One thing our generation is especially struggling with is how to discipline our kids. We are by and large against corporal punishment, but nothing equally powerful has risen up to take its place. So what you see is a lot of parents trying to reason with hysterical toddlers, or trying so hard to avoid saying a simple no that the message (no) gets totally lost in the "I'd really rather you didn't, because . . ."

There are few areas of parenting where one is liable to feel more judgmental of others, or more embarrassed later on when those same things we scoff about come back to bite us.

When Oliver was one and a half, there was this kid on the playground who was an absolute terror. He wouldn't share and he pushed other kids. He also snatched toys and pushed kids down. "No one will want to play with you if you keep that up," his father would tell him apathetically, without actually getting off the bench and making him mind.

A year later, he's like a totally different kid. His parents finally clamped down on his behavior, actually removing him from the park whenever he behaved badly, and he started at nursery school, where the structure agreed with him. The other day on the playground, he was the sweetest little boy ever. He shared his crackers with all the other kids and even gave them lessons in manners. "Uh-oh! That fell on the floor," he said in a sing-song voice. "Please go throw that in the trash, and when you get back I'll give you a new one." The stunned little girl did so and when she returned, he said, "Thank you! Here's a new cracker for you."

Like I said, totally different kid. Now his parents beam with pride.

Saying no, once you get used to it, is so satisfying. When Oliver went from being a baby (you can't spoil babies and they don't have a lot of freedom of movement, so there aren't a lot of no's in there) to being a toddler capable of sticking forks in light sockets and running out into traffic, no became necessary. It took some getting used to and I still find it hard sometimes.

The other day at the end of an episode of *Thomas the Tank Engine*, I said, "No more TV," because he'd been watching for a while and I thought he was starting to look kind of zoned out. I turned off the TV and was met with wails and pleas for more television. Inside my head, part of me was yelling, "He's crying! Make it stop! What's the big deal about another half hour? Who cares? The important thing is that he's sad! And for no reason!"

But the big deal was I'd already said no. To now cave in to his whining would be to set a dangerous precedent that if he screams and complains, he gets what he wants, and that "no" doesn't mean no.

I held firm, said no again, and went into the kitchen to start getting things ready for dinner. He followed me, wailing, but then he caught sight of a truck and went over and picked it up. Within a few minutes, it was like the tantrum had never happened.

Almost every choice when it comes to discipline is a tug-of-war between short-term and long-term benefits. Short-term fix: turn the TV back on. Long-term fix: endure the ten minutes of freak-out but cement the message that there are limits to TV watching and that when a parent says no to something, there is no negotiation. Also, we're the adults, and it's the curse of adulthood that we have to make the hard decisions, knowing full well that we'll get plenty of them wrong. One of the best parts of childhood is being spared the stress and frustration of decision-making. They don't know it, but they're very lucky it's not up to them yet to make the call that it's time to turn off *Dora* and eat dinner.

How Many Kids Should You Have?

Talking to my friend Tara, I said I thought Neal and I would have only Oliver. After all, I already have a great stepson, even if he's almost in college and we don't get to see him but a couple of months a year. He and Oliver are so great, it would seem like hubris to go for another one, like playing Blackjack, getting dealt "20" and saying, "Hit me!"

Tara, who has three children, scolded me for thinking of it like this. "You don't just keep having kids until you get it right," she said.

I realized there are a lot of reasons why we probably won't have more kids that make more sense than that I'm afraid of pushing my luck. Although frankly I understand people who have that fear—of having a second baby who is really hard work and muddles their relationship with their first kid. It happens. Of course, just as often an easy second baby follows an easy firstborn.

Everything's a crapshoot. You never know what you're going to get. And it's wussy to only want things to be easy. Neal's parents used to joke that they'd never have had Neal if his brother, Keith, had been born first, because Neal was really easy and Keith was a maniac. But of course they're both equally beloved.

Having a huge family is not the norm these days. The writer Katie Allison Granju has said

> *When I tell people I have four children, and that I would like to have more, the most common response is one of—for lack of a better word—distaste. . . . Many of the people I know personally who make it a point to actively support reproductive rights don't seem to believe that those rights should also extend to actual reproduction; this is especially true for pro-choice folks who seem to believe I am committing some kind of heinous eco-crime by giving birth.*

In an article called "The New Eugenics," Kara Jesella writes

> *According to the Population and Development Program at Hampshire College, industrialized countries, with only twenty percent of the world's population, are responsible for eighty percent of the accumulated carbon dioxide build-up in the atmosphere. The U.S. is the worst offender; in 2002, it was responsible for twenty tons of carbon dioxide emissions per person, compared to only 0.2 tons in Bangladesh, 0.3 in Kenya and 3.9 in Mexico.*[52]

She argues that it shouldn't be the obligation of individual women to have fewer babies, but rather to each household to limit its consumption, whatever the family size.

Anecdotally, I've noticed that having more babies seems to be way harder in the early years, when there are that many more diapers to change and new walkers to run after, and way easier later on, when they can entertain and look out for each other.

I think about Tara's kids, all of them brilliant and fun and funny, and I can't imagine any of them not being here. And I know if we had more kids, we'd feel that way about them, too. Each family is complete whenever it's done. "It's amazing, isn't it," our pediatrician asked on one of our first appointments, "how the second they're born it's like they've always been here?"

PART TWO

Food

On Food

My son asked for more juice. I filled up his cup with some diluted Mott's apple juice, and he returned to playing happily on the playground. But nearby children had heard the word: *juice*. They began to flock to us like zombies smelling brains.

"*Juuuuuuice!*" they wailed.

"No, honey, here's your water," one father said, thrusting a reusable metal water bottle into his daughter's hand.

My son offered the offending juice cup to his friends, but their parents quickly pulled them back.

"No, honey, juice is full of sugar," one mother stage-whispered to her whimpering little girl.

Several kids on our playground are allowed only water. Experts are behind this trend: *Parents* magazine has been railing against the evils of juice for decades.

My husband, raised in Texas on candy and soda, was baffled by this water purity. "What is this," he asked me, "*Babies in Alcatraz?*"

Juice contains empty calories; I get that. But isn't fruit supposed to be good for us? We dilute the juice so he gets the fluoride and all the goodness of water and also the flavor and vitamins. But all this no-juice purity makes me want to rebel totally and give my son a six-pack of Coke.

It's great that there's a move to more local and organic

foods, but in the frenzy to get everything organic, a perception has emerged that everything nonorganic is somehow evil. In fact there are only a dozen or so vegetables and fruits, such as strawberries and lettuce, that are really good to buy organic if you can afford to. According to the Environmental Working Group, there are plenty more where your pesticide exposure is negligible: avocado, banana, broccoli, and watermelon, for example.[1] Also totally not necessary to buy organic: pasta, cereal, bread, and fish. When it comes to organics, there are a lot more foods to not-worry about than to worry about.

At a birthday party Oliver and I went to recently, I noticed one of the kids—a healthy-looking kindergartener—had a brown-bread sandwich on her party plate rather than the cheese pizza everyone else was eating. *Lactose intolerance?* I wondered. *Tomato allergy?* Luckily someone else asked. Her parents explained: "She doesn't eat sauce."

She's not allergic. She just doesn't eat it. Sauce.

Whatever, I thought, *she's a picky eater. They want her to have a good time at the party and not rock the boat by trying to get her to eat what's served. Okay, path of least resistance. I get that.*

But the kid complained about her sandwich the whole time and asked for cake every two seconds. She whined and fussed and negotiated. How many bites did she have to eat? How about just one more? It went on for the entire lunch. Bringing the extra food had called a lot of attention to this very special child and had been, I thought, a bit rude, as the party throwers had gone out of their way to get something almost all kids love. And the worst part: both she and her parents seemed so stressed out by the whole thing. No one was having any fun. "We have to carry around special food for her everywhere," the father sighed.

Have to? Really?

In another instance, I was at a cookout one summer in the country. My son and a friend of his and a friend of that friend were playing nicely in the grass. When it came time for food, the father said to the boy, "No bun now with that hot dog." He had also warned the boy earlier that there was wheat in the crackers he was eating. Finally, someone asked, "Is he allergic to wheat or something?"

"No," the father said. "We just went to an acupuncturist who said he has a weak left kidney, and that the kidney has trouble processing wheat and so he shouldn't eat it."

There was an uncomfortable pause as the boy looked longingly at the hot dog buns.

"You look skeptical," the father said to one of the other parents.

"Uh, yeah," she said.

"Okay, you can have a half a bun," he told his son.

Later when the boy eagerly eyed some pasta, he was informed, "You already ate." When I raised my eyebrows, the dad said, by way of explanation, "Pasta has wheat."

Food in these cases seems so unnecessarily and so incredibly complicated. It seems for these parents to have a lot more to do with power and extra work and attention than it does about nourishment and socializing.

Another family I know was even more neurotic than the wheat-free one. The mother would say things to her son like, "What would you like to eat for a snack—carrots, avocado, or yogurt?" The boy would say, "Yogurt." Then she would make a pained face and say, "Oh, I'd really rather you didn't have yogurt. How about carrots?"

When it came to mealtime, she would change the rules

constantly. "You can't have dessert unless you eat your steak and potatoes. . . . Okay, just one bite of steak and two bites of peas. . . . No, three bites of peas . . . okay, one potato." The rules were so arbitrary and so hard to follow that it removed all incentive to do so. The kid would just push his plate away and look glum. I was with him: even a cupcake wasn't worth all that hassle.

Food should be fun. Or at the very least it shouldn't require such a lot of work. It's just the fuel a kid's engine needs. As long as you stoke the fire with decent-enough coal, the train's gonna keep a-movin'.

Defending Junk

When it comes to junk food, as in so many things, it really depends what kind of kid you have. Some kids will finish off a box of chocolate doughnuts if you turn your back on them for a second. Mine will eat all the sprinkles off a sprinkle cookie and then forget about it, or ask for a bag of M&Ms and then eat a few and run off to play.

So I like getting him treats, so long as he asks nicely. A polite request for a little shot of sugar in the late afternoon strikes me as eminently reasonable. Getting a "special treat," as he calls it, makes him happy and it makes me feel indulgent. And because he doesn't gorge, I don't have to feel like I'm ruining his dinner or his health.

Case in point: We were at the airport gate waiting for our plane. I took Oliver (at this point, two and a half) for a walk through the terminal. We went to the bathroom and to the newsstand, where I let him pick out a treat for the flight. He chose peanut M&Ms, which was convenient, because I like those, too.

"Chocolate, huh?" my father said when we got back to the gate. "He's going to be wired on the flight."

At that point, Oliver said, "Want one, Poppa?" and handed him an M&M. My father said, "Thank you," and Oliver said, "You're welcome." Then Oliver moved down the row and said,

"You want one, Daddy?" He repeated this until he'd given one to me, and my mother, too. Then he said, "I have one?" And ate one. Then he went down the row again and I said, "Can I have a brown one?" and he found a brown one. "I'd like two," Neal said, and Oliver counted out two M&Ms. "What color is this one?" my mother asked. "That's blue!" he said.

Talk about a dollar well spent. We killed fifteen minutes. Oliver wound up eating five M&Ms total. He got to practice identifying colors, counting, and manners. And he was very perky for the flight, but not a sugared-up maniac by any stretch. I was very proud of myself for having bought him the candy. I think there's something healthy about having that kind of enthusiastic but not obsessive relationship to sugar, one of our great human pleasures.

Besides, you know who the biggest sugar addicts are? People denied candy as kids. A woman I know who was never allowed sugar growing up now eats Three Musketeers bars by the fistful—and in front of her austere mother as often as possible.

Granted, there are limits.

One morning when I walked into the kitchen while visiting relatives in Texas, I found my four-year-old cousin pouring out a tall glass of Dr Pepper to go with her Froot Loops. When her grandmother came in, I expected the little girl to be scolded for trying to consume so much caffeine and sugar so early in the day, but instead Grandma said, "You better save some of that Dr Pepper for your little brother!" Her little brother was two.

But hey, those kids may have been a little buzzy those first couple hours of the morning, and they may have some cavities, but they are still totally healthy and charming. I'm of the bagel and cream cheese or French toast school of breakfast, but there are worse things, I learned that morning, than a seven a.m. sugar rush. Sure you crash fast, but that's what a midmorning snack of rice cakes and milk is for. Or, in my cousins' case, Snickers bars and Kool-Aid.

The everything-in-moderation school of thought on food is on its way back into vogue. Brett Berk, author of *The Gay Uncle's Guide to Parenting: Candid Counsel from the Depths of the Daycare Trenches*, recently wrote an article called "In Praise of Junk" in which he argued

> *Being a kid is extremely hard work. In fact, it's much like starting a new job every day: they're exposed to an onslaught of fresh information that needs to be integrated and acted on immediately; rules are often unstated or unclear, and then suddenly and righteously enforced; and their direct supervisors are often inexperienced, overworked, and incapable of delegation. Imagine yourself in that position. During your lunch break, or after each brutal day, don't you think you'd feel entitled to a quick burst of numbing relief?*[2]

Yes, there is an obesity problem in this country, I think due mostly to the fact that high-fructose corn syrup is in everything, right? So it's good to use junk as a special treat as long as you're eating real food the rest of the time. Food guru Michael Pollan's philosophy is "Eat food. Not too much. Mostly plants." As long as you stick mostly to that, there's definitely room for the odd package of Runts.

Booze and Drugs
(For You, Not the Kid)

I once edited a story by a woman who confessed to smoking pot to see her through a particularly brutal day at home with her toddler son. She described how she finds herself more patient, loving, and infinitely more fun to play Legos with when she smokes pot. She claims all these things make her a better mother to her toddler son—better able to enjoy him and to be a calmer, more affectionate mother to him.

I posted it on my AOL News blog and it immediately got 385 comments, about half of which said this woman was a terrible person who should have her kid taken away from her and the other half of which agreed that Mother's Little Helpers are just that, and that, by the way, pot is much better (less dangerous, less addictive, less toxic) than alcohol.

The article kicked up a sandstorm of controversy because it involved an illegal drug, but also because it voiced something that's usually left unsaid: there are days when it can be hard to enjoy your children. Sometimes on these days it helps to have a glass of wine, to leave your kid at the gym's daycare while you take a long shower, or to put *Elmo in Grouchland* on repeat.

I think people reacted so strongly because it came from a totally familiar place of wanting to medicate oneself in the face of one's child's demands. It's incredibly tempting. If I've had a long day at work and come home and Oliver's out of sorts, I am eager to grab a beer to nurse while I give him a bath. And just like in that pot story, it works for both of us. I'm more patient. He's got a playmate for that bath time classic "Shark coming! *Ahhhhhrgh!*"

Still, I'm very mindful that it's just one beer, and a lot of times I consciously skip it. There are a lot of alcoholics in my family, and I know just what a slippery slope it is from a beer here or there to that nightly bourbon or two or three, and before you know it you've checked out completely.

Yes, alcohol abuse paves the way for other kinds of abuse and car crashes and all that stuff, but more often than that what I see is that booze, or pot, or online poker, or work, or whatever else takes you out of the present. Your body is there, doing a puzzle on the couch, but your brain and heart aren't. Maybe kids can't tell, but what if they can?

Time to Eat

A friend of mine has totally given up on mealtimes. When it's time for her kid to eat, she just follows him around shoving food in his mouth when he pauses. He eats about three different foods total—pasta, hot dogs, and . . . Okay, maybe just two.

It really helps, I think, to set aside a time and place for food to be eaten. That may sound obvious, but it's harder to do that than it may sound. What's easiest is to follow kids around and shove food into their mouths.

That's fine and all if you never go out or see people, but if you like leaving your house or being around other people anytime in the vicinity of mealtimes, you want your kid to eat a wide variety of stuff, while remaining more or less still.

A common complaint among parents is that their kid won't eat anything but macaroni and cheese, or that each kid needs his or her own individual meal prepared, resulting in parents' cooking five different meals to satisfy everyone, and annoying logistics whenever a meal is taken at anyone else's house.

You want to be able to go to other people's houses without a cooler full of special food that the kid will actually eat. I think we can usually accomplish this by making only one meal, rather than special dishes for everyone depending on their particular whims that night. Kids eventually get hungry and will eat things other than hot dogs—unless there's a hot dog at every meal.

Still, for those of us who are not gifted at the culinary arts, it's hard to figure out other things to make, especially when you have only fifteen minutes between when you get home from work and when your kid goes ballistic from hunger. So I recommend getting together a bunch of incredibly easy ten-minute recipes and mastering a few of them. If you are a better cook than I am (which I promise you are), you can even get fancy and pre-prepare things and freeze stuff and all that.

I went the remedial route and recently got the Williams-Sonoma book *Cooking Together,* which is full of recipes you can make with little kids. It turns out this is my level of cooking ability, because I have aced the vegetable fritters, miniburgers, corn chowder, sweet potato fries, and snowball cupcakes. They all have very simple instructions and can be put together in a matter of minutes. I proudly showed off my latest creation to our foodie neighbor and he said, "Good for you!" Oliver looked at me with the same vaguely patronizing enthusiasm. Then he ate those veggie fritters all up.

A Modest Proposal:
Bring Back Home Economics

How did they ever let us take this baby home? More than one parent has wondered how they qualified to be left alone with their baby, not having any experience with children short of passing them on the street or having the back of an airplane seat kicked by them.

For some parents, their own child is the first newborn they've ever held, the first diaper they've ever changed, and the first infant they've ever bathed. No wonder there is a new-parent freak-out, what Susan Maushart in *The Mask of Motherhood* calls nurture shock: "There is no doubt that, whatever other changes new motherhood may entail, the neediness of the helpless newborn presents a woman with the ultimate test of her fitness to nurture."

It might be a little easier on new parents, both men and women, if they had some basic homemaking skills—not Martha-level, just a few simple recipes, the ability to sew on a button, to change a diaper, and to balance a checkbook.

And so I propose that we bring back home economics as a requirement for both girls and boys in high schools nation-wide. You can see this class being fun for everyone. One day you make chili; one day you try to grocery shop for the week on a $50 budget; one day some kindly members of the community bring their babies around and let everyone hold them. You can wrap sex education into this by casting safe sex and birth control as just more things you need to know about to be a responsible adult, not unlike how to boil eggs, how to change a flat tire, or how to call long distance.

Will this kind of schooling make us more competitive on the world stage? I would argue yes. Clearly, it's not calculus or a foreign language or physics, but it will help the future mathematicians and ambassadors and nuclear physicists to manage their home life and have healthy relationships, and thus be better able to do their work. Can you imagine how many people in American history, especially women, would have made major contributions to our culture if both they and their spouses knew how to make a nutritious dinner in fifteen minutes?

I am blessed to find cleaning pleasurable (or maybe *therapeutic* is a better word—after a frustrating day of work, scrubbing the bathroom floor is a way to get out hostility) and to have had babysitting experience, so I wasn't as freaked out as I might have been by the increased mopping demands and diaper changes that came with having a baby. But I still regularly stare into the refrigerator and fail to imagine a single thing I have the knowledge and ingredients to cook.

Why don't we learn in high school how to make chili, lasagna, tacos, vegetable curry, and a couple of other things? Why don't we learn how to take care of a cast-iron skillet? How to soothe a baby? How to properly clean a bathtub?

Well, probably because it's so closely associated with super-conservative '50s-style paternalism.

When I was a teenager, I got obsessed with old home economics textbooks. I found a bunch of them at garage sales one summer and delighted in reading them out loud to my mother and mocking them. I still have a bunch, and they're good conversation pieces at parties.

My favorite: *Young Only Once: Secrets of Fun and Success* by Clyde M. Narramore, Ed.D. (1957). Take these wise words from page nineteen: "There's nothing more wholesome than clean fun. . . . It makes you feel good afterward. True, many young people unfortunately indulge in what is often called fun but might better be labeled with the old-fashioned (and truthful) word sin. Never mistake sin for fun."

The book is handy for certain things: tipping, for example, and thank-you note etiquette. But unless you are planning a traditional Christian midcentury middle-class marriage with the husband off to work and the wife at home, there is nothing in here to help you feel anything but anxious and guilty about how easy it is to fall into sin when you're just trying to have a good time.

But home ec doesn't have to be that way. First of all, it doesn't have to be a girl thing. And beyond that, it doesn't have to revolve around a fantasy of a happy homemaker wearing an apron over her tulle skirt. It can revolve around a fantasy of a happy parent, partner, and citizen, someone who isn't *completely* blindsided by bank fees, an empty cooking pot, or the wail of a newborn baby.

Snack Attack

We don't fight that often, Neal and I, but we do argue plenty about the quantity of snacks that should be made available to our child. My reference point is being a hungry houseguest without knowledge of where the nearest store is or whether or not it's okay to just go into the kitchen and fry myself up an egg.

Children seem like that to me—utterly dependent house-guests—so I try to make it easy on them by putting out lots of little bowls of things—carrots, Ritz crackers, strawberries, popcorn—and by making sure the stroller is stocked with lots of baggies, too: Cheerios, pretzels, pieces of cheese.

"He's a growing boy!" I say. "He needs to keep up his energy!" Not to mention, hunger is his number one trigger for tantrums.

Neal says I am stuffing him like a *foie gras* goose and that he's going to grow up to be "husky."

I say he's strong and tall and thin, so whatever we're doing is working and that he should keep snacking, because he still eats his meals and he's superhealthy and he's not "husky" so far and so what if he was? He could be the first person in our families to play football.

Such are the totally stupid fights we get into. And such are the compromises that we now pack only one snack in the stroller and I restrain myself from asking every half hour if I should make some popcorn. Oliver is not a stranded houseguest. We live right around the corner from a very well stocked deli. If Oliver wants a little bag of pretzels, he can ask us to stop off there on the way to the park.

But when we go anywhere that doesn't have a deli on every corner, you'd best believe that stroller has about a thousand Ziploc bags, each one filled with some energy-giving, tantrum-preventing snack or another. Neal may scoff, but many an airline passenger on a grounded flight, fellow line-waiter, and wedding guest has been glad that our toddler had his choice between raisins, rice cakes, and Honey-Nut Cheerios. Having too many snacks may be a problem, but it is nowhere near as bad as not having enough.

Allergy Alert Days

Of course there is a flip side to being all whatever's-whatever about food, and so I warn: *Don't hand that hungry toddler on the playground a peanut butter cracker!*

Allergies to peanuts, eggs, wheat, and more are all over the place, and you could be sending others to the hospital just by being generous with your kid's snack.

Sometimes it takes even less than a cracker. Our friend's daughter tested something like forty on a scale from one to seven with a few allergies. When another child touched her after eating a peanut butter–and-jelly sandwich, she broke out in a hand-shaped rash!

The numbers are out of control. In early 2009, the National Center for Health Statistics reported that the number of children diagnosed with food allergies has increased 18 percent in the last decade.

And why?

A leading theory is the Hygiene Hypothesis, which suggests that Americans' hypercleanliness has weakened our immune systems to the point that something as seemingly banal as peanuts can send our bodies into a frenzied immune response.

Scott T. Weiss, MD, professor of medicine at Harvard Medical School, wrote in the *New England Journal of Medicine* in 2002: "Eating dirt or moving to a farm are at best theoretical rather than practical clinical recommendations for the prevention of asthma. However, a number of environmental factors are known to be associated with a lower incidence of allergic disease early in life."

Poor air quality and other environmental toxins seem to be a factor. We should be vigilant about these things and try to get cleaner air, especially for inner-city kids. There are definitely problems to address.

Even so, the paranoia about allergies is excessive.

"I've read conflicting things about when to start solid food," the mother at a café near my house told me, pointing to her (rather alarmingly pudgy and surly to my eyes) eight-month-old daughter, "so we're still just breastfeeding. Does your son eat solid food?"

This, of course, was a setup. There is no way you can answer such a question correctly. When a stranger says to you, "Does your son do such-and-such [sleep through the night, eat vegetables, nap, travel well, watch television, still wear diapers]?" she almost never wants to know.

In this case, she wanted to hear that I had started feeding him solid food at five or six months (which I had), so she could tell me that the *latest* research on the parenting blogs *she* read said you should put it off as long as humanly possible to avoid allergies. Which is what she did. She looked at her daughter like the girl was an A-plus science project.

This kind of developmental hauteur always makes me want to lie. "We started him at *six days*, actually. On *steak*." That, or do her one better: "No solid food for us! Breast milk either! With our boy, we're following a strict air-itarian diet—oxygen only. I mean, why take chances?"

But then Oliver ran over, gobbled a few handfuls of Chex

out of a Ziploc bag in the basket of our stroller, and blew my story.

Every time I am confronted with one of these researcher-parents, I wonder whatever happened to just doing things when your pediatrician says to? Good doctors have read all the research, or they've been in touch with the AAP advisory board, whose members definitely have read them all, and unlike us, they have zillions of years of education that lets them actually understand these studies and put them in context.

To believe that there is a vast medical-industrial conspiracy working overtime to make you do something that's bad for your kid is the height of narcissism. If you don't trust your pediatrician on the simple matter of when to start feeding your kid rice cereal, I wanted to ask this no-solid-foods mother, why don't you just find another doctor?

I also wanted to remind her that there is ultimately very little satisfaction to be had from testing out theories on your child. The results are always inconclusive. You'll never know if it was something you did or didn't do, because the variables are endless and there's no control group.

As a generation, we're obsessed with doing everything "right," but for 99 percent of the decisions a family makes, there is no definitive right. Wanting to be the perfect parent comes from a good place, but it's a waste of energy and sets up everyone for failure. You're not just a bad parent or a good one. There is a huge spectrum between a Stepford wife and a candidate for Child Protective Services. Almost all the parents I know are in between the two, and doing a pretty good job.

Having a baby isn't a test you need to get an A on or a project you have to complete and submit to a board for approval.

You just need to keep them alive and out of trouble and do what you can to ensure they develop into reasonably well adjusted people. Failing some kind of massive childhood trauma or mental issues, all of us are inherently—instinctively—up to this challenge.

And where's the pleasure in spending your children's early years generating and testing out pet theories on them? Render to the allergist what is his, and keep the other more exciting stuff for yourself.

The Evil Turkey Sandwich

For a few weeks when I was pregnant, all I wanted was a Subway turkey sandwich on Italian bread with lettuce, tomato, and mayo.

"No deli meat!" some of my weekly e-mail updates insisted, as did my pregnancy books. But I didn't care. I wanted that sandwich so bad. I started going to Subway every day at lunch. I got that sandwich and chased it down with lemonade, and enjoyed every bite. Maybe it was even tastier because it was illicit. I wasn't drinking martinis, but by God I could still have a vice: it was six inches long and had less than six grams of fat.

I must have Googled *pregnancy* and *deli meat* a million times seeking absolution, and every answer I found was more upsetting than the one before. My personal favorite, from Yahoo Answers, was this: "There is no need to worry about it if you have just eaten it. Don't eat anymore of it—but you don't need to worry. It can cause miscarriage, but only if the baby gets listeria from it. . . . It's not like everyone who eats it will get sick—you just don't want the risk. Nothing now to worry about, however."

Yeah, thanks a lot, I would think as I headed around the corner to Subway to guiltily consume another sandwich.

Eventually I got around to looking up how common listeriosis is, and learned that 2,500 people get it every year in the United States and 27 percent of those are pregnant women. It's really scary if you get it and it can cause miscarriage, but then I looked up how many babies are born every year in the United States: it's something like four million. The chance of it seemed slight enough to risk a little turkey a couple of times a week— okay, every day for a month.

But then, just like that, the craving was gone, and all I wanted was fruit. Fruit and yogurt. Constantly. Then it was waffles. Ice cream sodas. Grilled cheese. Mexican corn. Cereal. I stopped Googling foods because I was afraid I would be told not to eat them and I wanted them so, so badly. I was hungry all the time, even at night. I kept granola bars on my bedside table so I could eat them when I woke up at three in the morning, ravenous. And if I was somewhere that I couldn't get food, I would cry or leave.

One time my husband had to perform on a boat docked in the Hudson River. It was a benefit and dinner was supposed to be served, but the organizers screwed up and so there was only a bar. I thought I could make it the hour or two until Neal was done and we could leave, but after about half an hour I was so hungry I was about to start weeping, so I told Neal I was going to go look for dinner, descended the plank, and started walking. It took about fifteen minutes of power-walking along the river until I came upon a sports complex, located a bowling alley, and acquired a hamburger, fries, and a milk shake. It was one of the best meals of my life.

Yes, in the course of all this eating I gained a ridiculous amount of weight: almost sixty pounds. But I had a very healthy time of it all. My baby was almost nine pounds and I lost almost all of the weight in the first few months. And I enjoyed my pregnancy. Would I have been as happily pregnant if I had gained thirty pounds less, never had a turkey sub, not had that (very, very tiny!) sip of the super-old, expensive whiskey someone brought to a party straight from a cask in Kentucky?

Overall, I took exceedingly good care of my unborn baby. I ate balanced meals, took prenatal vitamins, didn't smoke or drink (except for that sip and about one glass of wine total). But I realized that I had to take good care of myself, too, which meant throwing away the fascistic *What to Expect* cookbook and (within reason) eating whatever I damn well pleased, even the nefarious turkey sub.

The Breastfeeding Wars

"Make a sandwich!" the lactation consultant instructed before she was called out of the room. Propped up on five million pillows, I squeezed my boob into a sandwich and tried to feed it to my hours-old baby. He couldn't latch, so he wailed. I cried, too. We both sat there sobbing. I felt like a failure and like my baby was going to starve to death in the minutes it was going to take for someone to come help me. Finally I got the consultant back in the room.

"Uh, you're trying to feed it to him vertically," she said. "Do you eat a sandwich vertically?"

In my delirium and weepiness, I had no idea what she was talking about. A vertical sandwich? It sounded like a band name. What kind of band would call itself Vertical Sandwich? Why were we talking about indie rock?

While I blubbered, the nurse grabbed my boob and sandwiched it the other way, pointed my nipple up, and pushed it into my baby's mouth. Voilà. He started suckling! He was happy. I wasn't in pain. "Thank you!" I called after her as she moved on.

And I'm proud to say it only took her and the other nurses groping me in this manner a thousand more times before I got the hang of it myself. I used to be shy about changing in communal dressing rooms. I didn't like to leave the bathroom door open when I showered even when there was no one else in the apartment. And yet here I was, being felt up by strangers every day, and I didn't even blink. Feeding that baby became the most important thing in the world, so much more important than not flashing medical personnel and visitors that I lost every last shred of modesty.

In the year that I nursed my child, there were bouts of pain, especially when I weaned, but overall it was kind of amazing to be able to generate food for another person. He thrived and grew fat, and was completely relaxed the second I took him into my arms. He would often fall asleep when I nursed him in the evening, and I would, too. It was like a wonderful drug we were both on.

But, of course, a lot about it was still annoying: I continued to be hungry all the time, almost as much as I had been during pregnancy, and if I drank less than about a gallon of water a day, my supply would dry up. It was frustrating not to be able to be apart from my baby for more than three hours at a time unless I'd pumped a bottle. I remember bursting into tears at my three-month midwife checkup because I'd left only one bottle back at home with my husband and I'd been waiting so long in the waiting room that I was sure he'd need another before I could return. (I also may have been a little sleepy.)

Oh, and then when I went back to work, there was so much pumping! I spent many, many hours in the bathroom at work listening to the *hiss-suck* of the pump while I filled up bottles to bring home for our freezer. It didn't hurt once I got the hang of it, and a hands-free bra (wow, are those nowhere near as sexy as they sound) let me read or write while being milked. But I lived in fear of forgetting to lock the door and being walked in on by some poor intern. And there was something kind of embarrassing about leaving Oliver with friends and a bottle of milk from my body. I'll never forget the look on a friend's face when he tipped out a drop of milk on his wrist to check the temperature and realized it wasn't formula. "Uh, yeah, that's my breast milk," I had to say. And he was all, "That's cool," but I still blushed.

Breastfeeding is really hard to keep going if you have anything else to do. It requires *a lot* of time. It kind of muddles your brain. It burns a lot of calories so you have to keep fortifying. It's a lot of pressure on the mother because the baby's sole source of fluid, food, and therefore survival is on her shoulders. As a result, men often feel left out— even while they're fancy-free to leave the house for more than the length of an action movie without first attaching hoses to their body.

I thought it was worth it, all things considered, but it's not worth it for everybody, or even possible for everybody. I have plenty of friends who tried desperately to do it and, with constant pumping, lactation consultants, medicines, and gadgetry, managed it for a couple of weeks or months. They did right by their babies' nutritional and immunity needs, but they were incredibly worn out by the ordeal and didn't get to enjoy new motherhood nearly as much as they would have if they'd just gone ahead and supplemented with formula.

Women who must, or choose to, feed with formula are often subject to condemnation by strangers on the street. One of the many, many crazy things about this is that just decades ago in the United States (when formula wasn't nearly as high quality!), women were encouraged to use formula rather than breastfeed. We now know nursing has many benefits and is ideal, but we can't forget that formula isn't poison, and it's a completely viable substitute if a substitute is needed for whatever reason.

Besides vaccination and circumcision, breastfeeding is probably the most controversial issue out there for new parents. It's the best way to feed a baby, hands down, but a million things can trip you up, from oversupply to undersupply to improper latch or thrush. Given the variables, the amount of pressure to succeed at all costs is insane. It's not like you can't bond with your baby or keep her nourished any other way. Especially if you have to work a lot or you have serious problems with the process, the stress of nursing can quickly outweigh even the tremendous health benefits.

Breastfeeding is the most natural thing in the world, but it's also a learned skill. Without a mother or grandmother around to show you how (and not a lot of women of those generations breastfed, so good luck), you need some really good nurses, books, or YouTube clips to get the hang of it. It's definitely worth trying, even trying hard. But it's not worth killing yourself over. Your job is just to make sure the baby grows and is sated and isn't orphaned by a mother who out of frustration strangles herself with her Pump In Style breast-pump tubing.

In an article called "The Case Against Breast-Feeding" in the April 2009 edition of *The Atlantic*, Hanna Rosin, who herself nursed three children, said that today's women are being held down by nursing the way women of the 1950s were by the vision of the happy housewife. She wrote

> *When I looked at the picture on the cover of [Dr. William and Martha] Sears's Breastfeeding Book—a lady lying down, gently smiling at her baby and still in her robe, although the sun is well up—the scales fell from my eyes: it was not the*

vacuum that was keeping me and my 21st-century sisters down, but another sucking sound.

Yes, she compares a nursing baby to a vacuum cleaner.

On one hand, I see what Rosin is talking about. Especially in a certain class of women (a video accompanying the article online showed Rosin and several friends luxuriating in a well-appointed living room), there is a lot of pressure to breastfeed at all costs—no matter how difficult it may be on a woman's body, career, or other relationships.

The growing "breast-free breastfeeding" trend of pumping rather than nursing directly is evidence that women are really knocking themselves out to breastfeed even if it's physically (or in some cases psychologically) all but impossible. I have friends who pumped every couple of hours the first few months of their babies' lives. If they did by chance get a free minute to nap or just cuddle their baby, out came their taskmaster, the *ka-thunk, ka-thunk* of the breast pump.

Rosin writes, "Given what we know so far, it seems reasonable to put breast-feeding's health benefits on the plus side of the ledger and other things—modesty, independence, career, sanity—on the minus side, and then tally them up and make a decision."

Whoa. Modesty? Since when is it immodest to nurse your baby? Even without the feeding thing, are you really so *independent* with a new baby you love and want to be around as much as possible? Shouldn't we try to reform the workplace to make it more conducive to new motherhood rather than just saying women should not feel any obligation to it?

And if her argument is really that you should just make up your own mind about whether or not to nurse your baby, why a story entitled "The Case Against Breast-Feeding?" After all, the AAP and WHO are concerned with public health. And for most women in most parts of the world most of the time, breastfeeding is the clear ideal.

Birth expert Jennifer Block (author of *Pushed*) believes "this breastfeeding backlash isn't so much about breastfeeding, but about the same domestic oppression that has been dogging mothers since the '50s, the women's movement notwithstanding. We seem to be taking this anger out on our own bodies (resenting the parts and processes that make us female, rather than demanding support from the culture). Is there such a debate over breastfeeding in, say, Sweden, where women are paid to be mothers?"[3]

Block makes a lot of sense. Rather than complaining to one another, or calling one another out for being too pro- or too anti- deeply personal things like breastfeeding, we should demand more cultural support for families to make whatever choices they want to make.

Eating Together as a Family

One evening when my son was about a year old, a delivery-man came to our door bearing dumplings and noodles. Oliver saw the bag in the man's hand, said, "Yum!" and ran for his high chair.

We had, apparently, trained him that the good food comes from bags borne by strangers. Out of some guilt, I started cooking more often, but I couldn't blame Oliver for getting excited about takeout. I get excited about it, too.

Our pediatrician isn't insistent about very many things, but when he told us to start trying solid foods at about five months, he said we should start eating together as a family then and keep it up for as long as our son lived with us.

"It may seem easier to feed the kid first," he said, "and then to have a grown-up dinner later, but that misses the point of meals. You want to check in with the family, and the child is part of the family. Better get used to that sooner rather than later. He's going to be with you for a long time."

This brings up larger issues of where your kids fit into your life. Some parenting books stress that the child must work around your schedule; others say the child should lead you and that your life should revolve around him. This is called child-led, versus parent-led, parenting, if you go in for the lingo.

When I went to see a friend's band play recently, I over-heard a woman I knew lecturing a pregnant woman on how to handle new motherhood.

"Show the baby right away who is boss," she said. "The baby has to fit into your life, not the other way around. We needed a baby who would sleep through anything because we're very social and have lots of parties at our house. And now he's six and very social and can sleep through anything. *They* will adjust to *you*."

What she said is true, of course. And it's good to keep in mind as a corrective to the most extreme attachment parenting, by which parents are yoked in constant service to their children. After all, how can someone totally dependent on *you* control your life without you letting him?

And it's good to keep in mind that everything about your life doesn't have to change. You can still have parties, for example. You don't have to become a shut-in. Babies don't care where you are. They just want to be held and loved and talked to and fed. They also need a lot of sleep. So there's plenty of wiggle-room in there.

But an extreme kids-will-adjust philosophy is just as damaging.

The epitome of the parent-led movement is evangelical preacher Gary Ezzo's bestselling *On Becoming Baby Wise*, published by the Christian publisher Multnomah/Questar. On the Web site parentwisesolutions.com, Ezzo describes his books as "more than an infant-management concept; it is a mind-set for responsible parenthood." Key to the strategy is feeding the baby when the clock says to rather than whenever the baby cries for food.

Dozens of healthcare providers sent a "letter of concern" to the AAP in 1997 suggesting that Ezzo's philosophy was dangerous to babies.

In a 1998 feature on Salon.com, Katie Allison Granju wrote a takedown of Ezzo's philosophy and documented many of the health concerns surrounding that parenting style. While Ezzo's infant-feeding advice has been most controversial, Granju finds his recommendations for older children even more shocking:

> . . . After babies reach only 6 months of age, parents are instructed to begin punitive disciplinary measures such as "squeezing or swatting" of the child's hands or "isolation" in the crib for "rebellious" infractions including "foolishness," "malicious defiance" or even playing with food on the highchair tray.

This is a pretty extreme expression of the idea of "parent-led" feeding and sleeping.

In the other direction, you have the attachment-parenting extreme represented by Dr. Sears. On his popular askdrsears.com, he describes the goal:

> Attachment means that a mother and baby are in harmony with each other. Being in harmony with your baby is one of the most fulfilling feelings a mother can ever hope to have. Watch a mother and baby who are attached (in harmony) with each other. When the baby gives a cue, such as crying or facial expressions, signifying a need, the mother, because she is open to the baby's cues, responds.

Sounds good, but there is dripping disdain for parents who go for some kind of middle ground:

Attachment parenting teaches you how to be discerning of advice, especially those rigid and extreme parenting styles that teach you to watch a clock or a schedule instead of your baby; you know, the cry-it-out crowd. This "convenience" parenting is a short-term gain, but a long-term loss, and is not a wise investment. These more restrained styles of parenting create a distance between you and your baby and keep you from becoming an expert in your child.

"You know?!" No, I don't know. Tell me about how I (and all the great parents I know who let their baby cry for a couple of nights so everyone could get to sleep) have "created a distance." This kind of haughtiness always makes me want to do the opposite thing. When I read a bunch of Dr. Sears, I want to put my two-year-old outside with $5 and a packed lunch and tell him, "Have fun, kid! Just be home for dinner!"

I totally understand why that whole Dr. Sears attachment-parenting extremism is so appealing, especially to parents of our generation, who were raised by distracted Baby Boomers. I also understand why we want to take our kids to sign language class, to play them the Ramones instead of Anne Murray, and to spend hours Googling seemingly innocent accoutrements like prenatal vitamins before we decide whether or not to allow them into our homes. We're overcompensating for too little attention with, very often, too much.

The truth, as the writer Madeline Holler says, is "hybrid systems aren't just for cars."[4] In my experience, it's best to take a little from column A, a little from column B. I used a sling and breastfed because it was convenient and pleasurable. I sleep-trained and used time-outs because we needed some structure and limits (and sleep). We have a happy kid who sleeps and eats. We love him more than anything in the world and genuinely delight in being around him. And we reserve the right to do whatever it takes to keep all those things true, no matter which side of the parenting aisle it comes from.

PART THREE

Love

On Love

When I was four weeks pregnant, I went to a Christmas church service. The little boy leading the choir stepped into the church and opened his mouth to sing the opening line of "Once in Royal David's City": "Once in royal David's city/ stood a lowly cattle shed/ where a mother laid her baby/ in a manger for his bed/ Mary was that mother mild/ Jesus Christ her little child."[1]

I promptly burst into tears and sobbed for two hours straight.

When we were putting the baby's room together a few months later, I had another two-hour crying jag, brought about by the *Guys and Dolls* song "More I Cannot Wish You" on the stereo: "But more I cannot wish you/ than to wish you find your love."

Uncle Arvide sings it to Sarah, who thinks she should marry a responsible, noble man rather than the gambler she's in love with. I wanted exactly that for my son, too: love and happiness and so much more. And he wasn't even born yet.

Another song that reduced me to tears: Mates of State's "Nature and the Wreck" ("I know we haven't said enough/ But I know I've never loved this much"), which has the sound of their baby cooing at the end.

In the midst of all the doctor visits and the crib assembly, it's easy to forget that the whole goal of raising our babies is to prepare them to leave us. Every new development stage, every inch they grow, they're that much closer to not needing us. It's usually some song that knocks that thought into my head (and the wind out of me), and I find myself sideswiped by this fact on a regular basis.

Like once, a couple of months ago, at a dinner party, someone told a story about having worked as a counselor at a camp for disabled kids. There was one boy there who had everything physically wrong with him a kid can have wrong, but who was extremely happy. Then one day, the counselor read a letter the boy's parents had sent their son. It read: "If we'd been given the choice of any baby in the world, we'd always only have picked you." He handed it to his cocounselor and said, "Quick, read this; it's the meaning of life."

My son is now almost three. Friends of mine with older kids smile knowingly whenever new parents like me wax philosophical, and they just roll their eyes at the racks of parenting memoirs or advice books written by parents whose kids are still in diapers.

They're right, of course—what do we know? But at the same time, I understand the glut of memoirs about pregnancy, about the first year of parenthood. Something about this sudden depth of feeling, the stab of happiness and sadness and hope and fear, feels like wisdom.

When he was a few months old, Oliver was with us at the Christmas service. After a few carols, he started to get a little fussy. An older woman in front of us turned around, and I was afraid she was annoyed. Instead, she reached her arms out and, without saying anything, just took him. She and the woman next to her immediately started making him fly between them and making faces at him. He laughed and seemed perfectly happy to be out of my arms.

I was so grateful to these strangers admiring and entertaining my baby, and so moved by the hymns (all of which—how had I never noticed?—are about a baby and his mother). But without all the pregnancy hormones surging through my body, I held it together and didn't cry.

Until I got home.

The Name Game

My best friends in first grade were named Jill and Amy. One day we realized we liked one another's names better than our own. So we traded. I was Amy, Jill was Ada, and Amy was Jill. For a day or two, we would only answer to our new names. I'm sure we drove our teacher and parents crazy. But I remember feeling like a totally different person while I was Amy. I felt cuter, and like life was suddenly a totally blank slate (even by first grade I had some neuroses). Anyway, I've since come to like my actual name, but that experiment in grade school made me more conscious of the power of a name to change your self-image.

When it came time to name my baby, I took it very seriously. Neal and I looked at books, looked online, and asked around for people's favorite names. We settled on a girl's name early: Veronica, after a writer and editor named Veronica Geng who had been really nice to me when I was a teenager and who had died far too young. We were going to give her Neal's late mother's middle name: Carol. Veronica Carol Medlin. It had a nice ring to it. And if she ever wanted to go into theater, Veronica Carol would be an especially cool stage name.

So of course we learned at the twenty-week sonogram that we wouldn't be having a girl at all. I mourned Veronica Carol.

Boys' names were harder. We were leaning toward the name Oscar, although Claude for some reason also appealed to us. (I think because we were watching a lot of old movies at the time and were kind of fascinated with Claude Rains.)

Then one night when I was six or so months pregnant, Neal and I were doing a reading at a bar in Chinatown. The hostess, the writer Amanda Stern, said, "I've named all my friends' babies! Let me name yours." We said sure, and she said, "I'm just going to ask you two questions: What is the last name, and what kind of name do you like: creative or traditional? We told her we liked something traditional but not something ten other kids in his class would have.

She looked at us for a second and then said, "Oliver."

I didn't like it at first, but said that was eerie because we'd been thinking about the similar name Oscar.

Later that week, I started to think of the name more. It had kind of a nice ring to it, actually. Neal and I tried it out while we walked around the city: "Oliver, come down off that recycling bin!" "Oliver, hurry up now!" "Oliver, want to stop in here for a cookie?" It fit.

Then Neal was on the phone to his dad one night and said we were thinking of Oliver for a name. "That's funny," my father-in-law said, "because that was your great-grandfather's name, and your great-uncle's name, and the name of lots of other people in our family." Neal never knew, because so many of his relatives went by their initials. Turned out O.N. was really Oliver Newton.

It also turned out that the Oliver Medlins were really cool.

The great-grandfather was a hobo even before the Depression, then became a traveling preacher and then married later in life, and very happily. Everyone remembered him as a great story-teller. That seemed like a good role namesake. And for the middle name we picked my mom's best friend, my beloved "Uncle" Gary.

I've read that the way to make sure you give a kid a name no one else he knows will have is to give him a name from your parents' generation, because those names always seem especially uncool. But the new trend these days is not only to not give kids names from your family, but to give them names that aren't actually names.

Increasingly popular is the practice of using nouns, like Rock, Tree, or Truck, as baby names. I was on the playground the other day and overheard this exchange:

"Oh, you had your baby! She's so cute! What's her name?"

"Pepper. What's your daughter's name?"

"Boulevard."

A writer I know named her daughter Fable.

Also encountered on the playground around the same time: a Tiger and a Ninja. Meanwhile, in the tabloids, we have the following celebrity baby names: Moxie Crime-Fighter, Pilot Inspektor, Zuma Nesta Rock, Kal-El, Jermajesty, and Kyd.

Kyd (Téa Leoni and David Duchovny's son's name) just seems like a combo of laziness and poor spelling, like naming your dog Dawg. At least the others show some creativity. So does the name Nevaeh, which is Heaven spelled backward and one of those freakish success stories that suddenly pop onto the radar of the Social Security Administration's addictive baby-name database.

I'm of the belief that it doesn't really matter what you name your child. They'll grow into the name, and any association you have with the namesake will be lost in your infatuation with the named.

When You're Pregnant,
It Takes a Village ...
to Judge You

A friend of mine recalls the worst thing anyone said to her when she was a new mother. She was at a cocktail party and carrying her baby girl in a sling. The baby was gnawing on everything—her mother's hands, her own fist, a pacifier, and a teether.

A drunk party guest said, "Wow, she's going to give a *great* blow job one day."

Does it get any more offensive? Well, most parents have a story that rivals it. It seems that people really don't know what to say when faced with a pregnant woman or with a new baby. But they feel that they must say *something*. Sometimes, what comes out is lovely and other times not so much.

One morning when I was nine months pregnant and on my way to work, two movers put down a dresser and beamed when I walked by.

"You're having a girl!" one said.

"No, a boy," I said.

"Positive?" he asked.

"Yes."

"Then you must be having twins," he said confidently. "The girl's hiding behind the boy!"

I really liked this game. It started when I crossed the line from awfully pregnant into obscenely, hugely, any-second-now pregnant. At least two or three strangers every day, entirely unprompted, would shout out "Girl!" or "Boy!" and I would call back "Wrong!" or "Right!"

I never stopped moving, so it added no time to my day. The exchange lasted exactly as long as a conversation on the street should last: the time it takes to pass by at a rapid clip. And it was fun playing quizmaster.

"Nope!" I told a woman behind the counter at a SoHo salad place when she said I was having a girl. "Damn!" she said, "I should have known! Everyone's having boys this summer."

"A boy, actually," I told an old woman at the recreation center on Carmine Street. She grabbed my stomach. "Ah, yes, a boy," she said, nodding sagely.

"How did you know?" I asked the ones who got it right. "You go across, not out," said the woman at the deli counter, proudly.

"You're carrying in the hips," said a random woman on the street.

"You're carrying high," said an old guy on my block, boasting from his stoop.

"Because you look pretty," said my friend Pailo at a party. I liked that one until I heard the rest of the prognostication: "In Mexico, we say a pregnant woman who looks bad is having the beauty sucked out of her by her daughter. If the woman glows, like you, it's because she has a penis inside her."

Which brings me back to the topic of grossly inappropriate things people say to new and expectant mothers.

My husband and I thought about waiting to tell people for the recommended twelve weeks, but at six weeks we were at a bar one night with some friends after a show of my husband's and someone asked me what I wanted to drink. "Just a seltzer," I said.

Immediately, twenty well-plucked eyebrows were raised in my direction. "Yes, I'm pregnant," I said when they wouldn't stop staring. Our friend Bridget, a singer, screamed and hugged me. "For some reason, I'm so happy for you, even though I can't stand it when most of my friends have kids!" she said. She was wearing an "Abortion Rocks!" T-shirt.

"You're so brave," said Earl, a producer, looking dour. "I mean, aren't you worried about bringing a child into such a fucked-up world?" Then he tried to get me to write an article about a show he was promoting.

I e-mailed a few friends I hadn't talked to in a while to tell them the news.

Jesse, a friend from high school, didn't write back at all. When I ran into him a couple of weeks later, he hugged me and said, "I was so excited I didn't know what to say."

"Congratulations?" I suggested.

Seriously, isn't that the default? One of those rules, like Miss Manners's rule that all brides and babies are beautiful?

Apparently not.

At a bar in the East Village before a friend's show, an acquaintance who was working that night handed me a couple of drink tickets. "Thanks," I said, "but I'm afraid you'd be wasting them on me." "Why?" he asked. I pointed at my stomach. "I'm pregnant." "Oh!" he said, and snatched back the tickets, then offered no further comment.

Two friends said congratulations, then immediately launched into stories about their miscarriages, one of which was at twenty weeks. I'd had no idea such a thing regularly happened, and it condemned me to spend eight more weeks than the usual twelve feeling as if losing the baby was still a possibility.

"You're not finding out the sex, I hope," said another friend when I told her about the baby-to-be. "I guess we will," I said. "It's harder not to find out. I don't think I'd be able to look away from the sonogram." "But you must!" she said. "It's terrible to know. You start projecting things onto the baby right away. You shouldn't name the baby until after he or she is born for the same reason."

It was then that I learned people who have kids themselves often have very strong feelings about whether or not to find out the sex, and how to balance work with parenthood, and every other topic imaginable.

"When are you starting maternity leave?" asked a family friend when I was seven months pregnant. "I guess when my water breaks," I said, feeling chipper.

"Oh, you should take at least two months off before the baby is born," she said.

"But I love my job," I said, "and I feel fine."

"You won't feel like working at eight months," she said, "believe me." That wound up not being true, but for weeks I did wonder whenever I woke up feeling less than 100 percent if it was the beginning of the end.

Finally, my friend Stephen, a painter, won the award for

most appalling reaction. We hadn't spoken in a few months—he lives in Indiana and works as an electrician; we used to work together at a dating-service photo lab in Texas—so I was very excited to catch him up. "We're having a baby!" I said, happily. After a long pause, he said, "Wow. I just never pictured you as a mother."

Stephen later said he did not in fact consider me unfit, but was shocked that someone he still thought of as the town tramp could be a parent. "I still think of you as single and kind of crazy. I can't see you wearing anything but heels," he said, sadly. "Why would I stop wearing heels?" I asked. "I just don't know any mothers who do," he said. I told him that women in New York did actually have babies and still behave in a trashy fashion, which he found comforting.

Having a kid means so many things to so many people. If you live a frustrated life in the suburbs, like Stephen, it symbolizes the death of cool. For city-dwellers who rely on one another as family substitutes, their friends turning nuclear can seem like a betrayal. For people who already have kids, their friends' procreating can be a threat to the way they themselves chose to do things, as if working through the fortieth week or finding out the baby's sex somehow challenges the validity of the choices they made.

Luckily, everyone gets nine months to get used to the idea of a new baby. By the time my due date came around, everyone seemed excited. "We have some boy clothes for you," the anti-sonogram friend e-mailed me, having reconciled herself to the fact that we went ahead and looked at the screen.

Of course, now that I'm a parent, the inappropriate comments are on a whole different order.

One day at a playground near our house, I met a woman with a baby close to the same age as mine. Oliver was about nine months old, strong, healthy, happy, and pulling himself up on everything.

She and I chatted about how cute each other's kids were, and then she asked what my son's name was.

Her chirpy response when I told her: "Oh, we knew a baby named Oliver." Then she grew conspiratorial and whispered, "But he died."

I stared at her for a second, hoping she was making a sick joke.

Finally, I said, "Uh, I hope our baby will live?"

"It was so sad," she replied, totally serious.

And would you believe a year later when I was introduced to her again on the playground, she told me the same story! I wondered how many parents of Olivers she'd tormented with that story in the intervening months.

When I got married, I learned a lot about my friends that I didn't know before. I discovered some were incredibly supportive and grown up and fun. They RSVPed early and partied late. And they seemed genuinely happy for me. I learned that others were not there when push came to shove. They railed against the institution of marriage without ever asking why we'd chosen to get married. They made it all about them. One friend even said he was coming and then bailed out the day before because he decided he didn't want the hassle of driving two hours.

"It's amazing, isn't it?" my friend Logan said. "When you get married, the best wedding present you get is the knowledge of who your true friends are."

Having a baby also separates the wheat from the chaff.

I keep this in mind whenever a friend tells me she's pregnant. I say how happy I am for her, how wonderful it will be. And I try to channel the spirit of all those nonneurotic strangers on the street who greeted my pregnancy with nothing but the greatest curiosity and the purest delight.

A Reality Check
for Working Parents

Whatever we do, we are running afoul of some philosophy, some book, or someone's arbitrary standard of perfect parenting. If we both work full-time and have a babysitter, we are heartless, missing out on the best years of our child's life. If one of us stays at home full-time, that parent is sacrificing his or her (usually her) social value, future earning potential, and creative soul.

Fortunately, there is a growing support network for those who stay home with the kids. There are thousands of books out there about stay-at-home parenting, many of them with titles about "staying sane" and "managing the transition" and "reveling in the chaos." In the much-maligned *To Hell With All That: Loving and Loathing Our Inner Housewife*, Caitlin Flanagan praises her stay-at-home mother and suggests that her generation is too lax on the home front.

Of course, there's also plenty out there condemning the "SAHM," as she is now called. Books such as *Get to Work . . . And Get a Life, Before It's Too Late* by Linda R. Hirshman and *The Feminine Mistake: Are We Giving Up Too Much?* by Leslie Bennetts argue that women need to make their own money and be a part of the working world rather than staying home with the kids. Such books caution women that they are making themselves vulnerable to poverty in case of a divorce and that they are setting women's equality back. (No pressure, ladies!)

Okay, you may reasonably think after reading all of these books, *I can find a middle ground, a happy medium involving sharing work and childcare with a partner! Sure, we'll make a little less money, but we can make it work!*

Alas, trying to set this up is an uphill battle. Employers should be supportive of work shares, of flextime, of telecommuting. And yet so often they act as if the employee is trying to put something over on the company.

And even if such an ideal situation is achieved, it is rarely an easy fifty-fifty split immediately embraced as fair by both parties. There is just so much more total work when a baby is involved. So someone is usually doing more than they feel they should, feeling resentful and bitterly exhausted, and taking it out on the other.

The writer Hanna Otero wrote of her arrangement, in which she worked and her husband took care of the kids: "Unable to confront our frustrations honestly, Eric and I found ourselves going to head-to-head over weighty issues such as whose turn it was to unload the dishwasher."[2]

The guilt involved in these kinds of negotiations can be unbearable. I went out after work once to a play and sat there weeping in the dark because I felt so bad that I hadn't seen Oliver all day and wouldn't get home before he fell asleep. I can't remember a thing about the play now, but I know I didn't enjoy a single second of it.

Some people will say you *should* feel guilty for being away from your child. Your baby wants you around those first few months for sure, especially if you're breastfeeding.

But thanks to the way our culture is set up, not everyone can afford to, or wants to, take that first year, or first five years, or however many, off. So, many of us wind up doing this crazy juggling act. That we manage to get it done—raise our children, keep our jobs—is a miracle owing much to our do-or-die spirit, and very little to a culture that pays lip service to the family while making it extremely hard to take care of one, especially in a rough economy.

Very little has made me feel better about all this, but one thing that did is Dr. Penelope Leach's 2009 book *Child Care Today: Getting It Right for Everyone*. Leach was the codirector for the largest study of childcare in the history of the UK. She followed 1,200 families for four years to come up with a thorough and objective report on the advantages and disadvantages of each form of care (mother, father, grandparent, daycare center, preschool, nanny, etc.).

Her ultimate verdict? She says, with no small amount of authority, that each family ought to select the kind of care that best fits its own unique situation. Her research in a nutshell: the quality of care matters much more than the kind of care. That such a straightforward, nonjudgmental book should be so revolutionary is a sign of how polarized we've become.

I called her up at her home in the UK for still more reassurance, and she delivered.[3] Here is some of what she told me. I'm just going to quote her in the hopes that you find it as helpful as I did:

ON MOTHER CARE:

"You still end up with people seeing mother care as the gold standard and everything else as being lesser, whether that's care by the father or something else. In my own study we had 1,200 families and there were some pretty awful full-time mothers among them! The truth is, it depends. Who are we talking about? What mother? What family? What child? That's why I don't think there's a lot to be said for generalizing. People say to me, 'What kind of care is the best for a baby?' And really the best I can do is to give certain indicators of high-quality care. It just depends."

ON STAYING AT HOME VS. WORKING:

"I came out of this study feeling very strongly that this is one area in life where choice is absolutely vital, and where women in particular have a right to choose. They have to choose. Their ability to choose is what ensures the baby's care will be good, whether that means staying home or going back to work. What's bad is when the mother wants to go back to work but can't find childcare, or the other way around, where she desperately wants to stay home but can't afford to."

ON THE BABY FORGETTING YOU IF YOU WORK:

"I was rather shocked in my own research by how many parents genuinely believe that if they find a really good caretaker for their child, the child might come to love the nanny more. That is one of those rare cases where we can actually say, 'No chance. Not going to happen.' Unless the parent is separated from the child almost entirely from the very beginning, it just doesn't happen. It's actually quite surprising where children have had nannies for years, parents worry that when the nanny leaves the children will be terribly upset. And actually as long as everything remains stable with the parents, they're really not very. Yes, they're sad to see her go, but she's not the center of their world."

I've said before that I hate advice-driven parenting books, but Penelope Leach's new one is actually a policy reference book, put together to provide facts for those creating legislation for working parents, and it's really valuable.

The Leach book drives home just how much the rules have changed with this generation: There used to be a network for families. Now we are so independent, we have nobody to help us. We're all alone.

Our culture denigrates the family and makes it extremely hard to balance work and home, unless "you are singularly gifted: a highly qualified mother with a loving grandmother living around the corner, a devoted husband who wants to be involved, and a very understanding boss who will do anything rather than lose you," says Leach. "Unfortunately, that isn't a large percentage of us."

"You can't count on anyone," my friend Tara says during my pregnancy when I ask her if I should plan on family and friends to pitch in. She doesn't usually talk like this. She usually says things like, "Everything will be fine!" But on this subject she says: "Everyone says they're going to babysit, but they never do. Trust. No. One."

She was right, tragically right—only with small, surprising exceptions. During Oliver's babyhood, my mother helped out a lot, especially when Neal was out of town. One couple we knew did babysit a few times when Oliver was tiny and not that many other people trusted themselves with him. Another couple of neighbors stopped by often to hang out with Oliver and talk to us while we did the dishes. A few friends would come over for dinner while Oliver slept in the next room. We made friends in the neighborhood we never would have met otherwise.

No, we didn't instantly have reliable help. People helped when they wanted to, not necessarily when we most needed it. But we learned to rely on each other—and on ourselves.

Here's to Babysitters

Finding someone you trust with your child is magic. It's so much easier to work or do whatever you need to do when you know that your kid is safe and maybe even having fun. I'm always astounded by how much people tend to take their sitters for granted, or to criticize or complain about them.

Right out of the gate, we were so lucky. I was working a couple of days at home and Neal was home most of the time, too; in a pinch we could often rely on my mother, and occasionally I could lure an intern home from the office with the promise of free takeout and $12/hour so we could go to the movies. But after a year, it started to be really hard to do all the work we needed to do without some hours each week where neither of us were with Oliver. We decided we needed about ten hours a week of help.

We put an ad up on the site Craigslist for a part-time babysitter and got a ton of responses—three of which seemed great. We interviewed all three, and they all seemed nice, but the third, Erica, was special. We liked her instantly and were so comfortable with her. Oliver felt the same way. We could tell because he emerged from his room, saw her, and toddled over to put his head on her legs. She pulled him up into her lap and they sat like that for the rest of the interview. He just beamed at her. It was love at first sight.

She's been babysitting for him ten or fifteen hours a week since then. In that time, Erica has graduated from college with a psychology degree, gotten another part-time job, and moved twice. Meanwhile, Oliver has gone from a babbling new walker to a full-on preschooler who speaks in complete sentences, can climb anything, and has a bunch of little friends. He and Erica have been to museums, made their own play dough, and done a thousand puzzles. She's changed his diapers, fed him macaroni and cheese, and hugged him when he's fallen down. And all we had to do was pay her a few hundred bucks a month? It doesn't seem like enough.

We've done everything we can to keep her. We get her theater tickets, throw extra money at her whenever we can, and try to convey at all times how grateful we are that she's in our lives. And we make sure Oliver is as well behaved as possible to make her job easier (and ours, too, of course).

I was heartened when I was telling Erica the other day about what Oliver's teacher said about him. It was so nice I kept waiting, I said, for Miss Rachel to be like, "But . . . there is the biting and pyromania."

To which Erica, horrified by my very suggestion, shouted, "No! There is no 'but'! He is perfect!" She looked at him adoringly.

And I thought, *Marry me.* She loves our kid to the point that she defends him against hypothetical criticism. How did we ever deserve such a saint?

This is why I find nanny cams and those sites like isawyournannyblogspot.com so gross. I understand the anxiety that goes with leaving your child at home with someone else, and the desire to keep control even in your absence. I pack ridiculous amounts of snacks and make sure the house is clean and that Erica has every phone number I could ever imagine her needing and enough spending money.

But ultimately I don't expect her to follow any of my suggestions about food or activities. Hanging out with a kid requires lots of flexibility and winging it. If you don't have total faith in the person you're leaving your kid with, that's not good. You need to trust your pediatrician and your babysitter, and to find new ones if they seem shady.

And you can tell, can't you? If your child is unhappy with a babysitter, if he's hungry and grouchy and groggy when you get home—probably there's something wrong. But if he's happy and seems to be attached to the sitter, then chances are everything's okay. And it's also okay if the sitter does stuff differently than you do. I think Erica gives him a snack later than we usually do. They often take a ton of toy trucks to the playground whereas we take only a couple. They still sometimes go to this kid playspace we've pretty much written off.

It's amazing how much you can learn from sitters, like that the kid playspace doesn't suck as hard as we thought it did, or that two p.m. is in fact the optimal nap time (we'd still been trying to put him down right after lunch). It's also good for the kid to realize that different people have different techniques and that not every day is going to roll out exactly the same.

And yet, there's so much in the media about a tug of war between mothers and nannies. I've received countless pitches along the lines of: "How do you talk to your nanny?" as if she were an exotic, dangerous creature whose delicate psyche must be carefully managed lest she destroy your child from spite. I've even heard talk of "nanny coaches," who essentially function as couples' therapists for mothers and babysitters.

A nanny *coach*? If you need a coach to talk to your babysitter, something is wrong. If you didn't like what your sitter was doing, why wouldn't you just hire someone else instead? Or, I don't know, roll with it? As long as the kid is happy and you're getting to do what you want to do during those hours, it seems like no major harm is being done and you should just enjoy your time away from home.

We love most all of the babysitters on the playground. One particularly great group of women together take care of a small army of children. We've never met some of these kids' parents, whereas we see their children every day. At first, I was sort of critical of those parents who were missing out on such a massive amount of time with their kids. Who were these parents who had totally given over their children's upbringing to these other women?

But then, gradually, I started meeting the mothers and learning what they were doing while their kids were riding scooters around the park. One had taken off two years to be with her kids full-time and just that year had gone back to work running a major company. She was overwhelmed by the return to work but still trying to sort it out. She seemed really nice and to really love her kids. And she seemed to have a lot of faith in her babysitter to hold down the fort in her absence. And she was right to; her babysitter was awesome, and the kids were flourishing under her care.

I met another one of the mothers one weekend afternoon on the street and she was curious about what her son was doing all day. I told her who I thought his best friends on the playground were (my son and a couple of others) and what games they played (that week, piling on the same bike and seeing how far they could ride like that). I also said I thought his babysitter was wonderful.

Of course he'd always love his parents and they would still be the key influence in his life, but that sitter was doing a really good job subbing for them those fifty or so hours a week. She was strict but loving and her charge knew exactly where he stood with her. She cared about him but she didn't let him get away with anything. He was good at sharing, wonderfully chatty, and kind to younger kids, and it was largely to the babysitter's credit.

Some of the parents on the playground who were there every second with their kids were inconsistent, short-tempered, and didn't pull off nearly the sitters' results. I got the sense a lot of them were around their kids not because they wanted to be with them every second, but because they would feel guilty being away from them.

"Don't worry about it!" I wanted to tell them. "Your kid would be totally happy right now if a babysitter were pushing him on the swing and you arrived home in the evening excited about seeing him."

There's a lot to be said for being around your kids as much as possible, especially when they're tiny and craving their parents' love and touch, but there's also a lot to be said for finding good people who can fill in when you can't be there. There's no shame in admitting you need help and finding it, whether you have to be away from your kid to make money or to keep your sanity or for any other reason. The only shame is in not realizing that people who take good care of your children are heaven-sent and should be treated like the angels they are.

Birth Stories

The cover of the Life section of a local newspaper in a town in Florida I was visiting had a piece about "etiquette for mothers." One of the items that caught my eye instructed us to keep all details of our labor and delivery to ourselves. The advice lady said that you should remain silent about details, and if pressed, should respond, "Well, the end result is my marvelous child." If someone starts talking about their labor, you should make your excuses and leave the conversation.

This strikes me as both insane and impossible. How can you not discuss such an intense experience with other people who have been through similar but inevitably unique trials? It's like getting a bunch of people who swam the English Channel together in the same room and instructing them not to mention water, swimming, or Britain.

I know the grisly details about the labor of pretty much every fellow mother I've so much as pushed a swing next to, and I'm grateful for the information. In fact, I wish I'd heard all those stories before I'd been in that situation so I would have had more diverse accounts than those from our hospital childbirth class, TLC reality shows, and the (mostly pretty crunchy and/or terrifying) labor stories I turned up online.

As it turned out, I had pretty much the most medical birth you can have. I took the birth class and was totally ready to do a natural birth, but circumstances intervened. My midwife lost privileges at the fancy hospital I had planned to use, so at eight months along I was switched to a smaller hospital with less of a setup for laboring naturally.

Oliver still hadn't dropped after eight days post due date. My midwife induced with Pitocin, which makes contractions much more intense. I lasted a few hours on them, walking around the bed while hooked up to monitors and leaning over pillows when it hurt, but finally the pain was so intense I thought it might be good to get an epidural. I was at six centimeters.

The epidural guy, unfortunately, managed to jab my bone with that huge needle. This is the single worst pain I have ever experienced. I screamed so loud Neal said he almost rushed in from the hallway, where he'd been sent to get snacks, and decked the anesthesiologist. Once that was over and the drugs were flowing, I felt much better. I even took a nap. But when I woke up: still six centimeters.

At one point, an alarm went off. A nurse ran into the room and turned me on my side, then put an oxygen mask on my face. "What's happening?" I asked, but they didn't answer me until I'd been repositioned and breathed in some deep breaths. It turned out the baby had been pressing on the cord. The baby's heart rate had slowed down. Then, just as quickly, the alarm stopped and his heart rate went back to normal.

Hours rolled by.

My water was broken. I was walking around. And nothing. After twelve hours of labor in the hospital, my midwife said she thought we had to get the baby out. Not wanting to go through another panic of the baby's heart stopping, I was all for it. I was wheeled into the operating room.

C-sections require a pretty weird setup. You're laid out on a table shaped like a crucifix and strapped down. A curtain is placed below your neck to cover up all the gruesome doings down there. Your anesthesiologist stands behind your head, and your partner close by him.

There are a million doctors and nurses around. It's freezing. They make sure you can't feel anything and then they cut through all the layers of muscle and fat and everything to pull the baby out. Then they lean really hard on your chest (one of my ribs got cracked!) and push the baby out.

"The cord's around his neck," someone said.

"His head is wedged in here," someone else said.

"Wow, what big hands and feet!" the nurse I was friends with exclaimed.

And then I heard him cry. It was such an amazing sound: my son, crying. It didn't sound like I'd imagined it. It felt like ages before I actually got to see him rather than hear him.

When they finally brought him around and handed him to Neal, who held him down so I could see him, he didn't look like I'd expected, either. He wasn't a generic baby. He had so much character. He looked so *specific*. I started crying, and, because I was flat on my back, the tears just welled up in my eyes until they dripped down the sides of my face.

It was the most incredible, weird, magical moment of my whole life.

A lot of parents don't bond with their babies right away. I can see why. Newborns are crazy looking and mysterious, and their entrance into the world is a total shock to the system and often a cause of extreme pain. For every new parent who looks into her baby's eyes and falls instantly in love, there is another who looks at her newborn and sees a squishy stranger. It seems normal to me that it would take some time.

And yet, I immediately fell for Oliver. He was so curious—trying to open his eyes and look around even through the eye drops. He totally took everything in stride. I really admired that. If after the shock of suddenly breathing air and seeing light and being enveloped in blankets rather than amniotic fluid, he could be such a good sport, I figured I could be, too.

Labor Plans and Realities

Home birth and natural delivery classes are proliferating, even as C-sections are on the rise.[4] The disparity between what women think they should do to have their babies and what women wind up doing has never been greater. I believe the goals of labor should be getting a healthy baby and not dying in the process. The rest is truly up for grabs.

An old friend of mine called me when she was pregnant to discuss her birth plan. Oliver was a few months old at the time and I'd all but forgotten my labor and delivery by that point. I confessed to not having had much of a birth plan and told her what happened with Oliver's heart rate changing and the cord being around his neck.

"I'm determined to have a natural birth," she said. She had good reasons for wanting one: because she'd had back surgery, she couldn't have an epidural. If she couldn't have the baby naturally, she'd be knocked out and given a C-section. Also, she wanted a whole bunch of kids, and knew that it was hard to have a natural childbirth after a C-section (a VBAC).

And yet, there was something about the way she was talking about her upcoming labor that suggested she was obsessed with the whole idea of natural childbirth as an important personal experience. She quoted articles about "lost obstetric knowledge" and decried the medicalization of American life.

I said that was all well and good and I was sure she was right, but asked her to promise me that if her doctor said she needed a C-section she would listen. She wouldn't promise. She said she was dead-set and knew she could do it. She'd hired a doula. She had the breathing lessons down pat. She would not fail!

I said, "Just remember. You want a baby out of this. The baby's more important than you getting the labor of your dreams."

She called me a couple of weeks after her baby was born.

Apparently she was in agonizing, unmedicated labor for two sleepless days before labor stalled and she was told she needed a C-section. She resisted, said she had to keep going—and did for a while, she says—but then remembered our phone call and gave in. The next thing she knew she was waking up from the anesthesia and being handed her healthy baby. And it wasn't any less beautiful a moment than she'd dreamed.

I edited a story once by a writer named Tova Mirvis we called "In Praise of the C-Section."[5] She wrote this of her three C-sections:

> *If I've learned anything in ten years of motherhood, it's that the way our children are brought into the world means very little for how they live in the world. Nor do the intense hours in which we become mothers shape the months, years and decades of our actually being mothers. And if the experience of childbirth is in fact a crucial process, then let it be the process of teaching us that our children will emerge in ways varied and complicated, not necessarily in times or manners of our choosing, neither made in our image nor as proof of*

our prowess. Let birth remind us that, with children, so little goes according to even the most well drawn plan.

Dozens of people commented. Some pitied her and women like her. One woman wrote that she felt sad for anyone who wound up with a C-section, because natural birth is "a transformative, amazing experience." Another wrote: "I was brainwashed by the Bradley method and an incompetent midwife into having a horrible first birth that was almost fatal for me. Trust me, natural childbirth is not always transformative, magical, or empowering. Sometimes it leaves you with PTSD (literally)."

Tons of women discussed how they came to have C-sections, or why they chose to go that route rather than risk labor. I was struck by how totally different one delivery is from another. There's just no predicting how it will turn out and ultimately as long as the mother and baby come through the labor relatively unscathed, any type is a success and should be treated as such.

The *femachismo* attached to avoiding pain relief is getting tiresome.

Kathryn J. Alexander—coauthor of *Easy Labor: Every Woman's Guide to Choosing Less Pain and More Joy During Childbirth*—writes of virulent natural-birth advocacy: "This claim by the experts that women become better people, possibly even better mothers, for having successfully given birth without the benefit of medical pain relief, led me to wonder what excruciating physical challenge my husband should triumph over to become a superior father—and would I get to choose?"[6]

Not having had a natural childbirth myself (except for the dozen or so hours of labor before the epidural), I don't know for sure that I wouldn't be a natural birth advocate if I'd pushed my son out rather than had him removed from my abdomen. But I like what Alexander has to say on the subject: "I don't doubt that, for some women, natural childbirth provides an emotional boost that is powerful and gratifying. But for me, giving birth was the fulfillment of a lifelong wish to have a baby, not a means of self-actualization. The real adventure began when I became a parent."

Real Abuse

These days, everything is called child abuse. I have heard the term applied to bottle-feeding, sleep-training, and circumcising.

But it's sick to use that expression for anything other than genuine abuse, which is a whole different matter.

Recently I was at the playground with Oliver feeling somewhat sorry for myself because Neal was out of town and our friends had bailed on hanging out with me and Oliver, and he'd just stopped napping, so I had a huge, breakless stretch of baby time with no adult company.

Luckily, Oliver started playing with a kid on the playground whose father seemed similarly at loose ends. We wound up talking for an hour while we followed our kids around the park. It turned out he worked with disabled high school kids: ED or MR, emotionally disturbed or mentally retarded.

"But most all of the kids I have right now are both," he said. "Like this one kid. His mother is in prison and his father is dying of AIDS. He lives with his grandmother, who's in her seventies. And every once in a while he beats her up."

"Jesus," I said, "how do you do it?"

"It's harder making the transition back home," he said. "As soon as I get home, my wife goes to work and I wish I had just a half hour to decompress before taking over with him." He pointed to his two-year-old son.

It reminded me how incredibly lucky I and Oliver and all our friends were. When we talk about being bad parents, we talk about letting them watch a lot of TV or eat a bunch of junk food or we waffle on discipline or bedtime or something like that. But these are very small things in the grand scheme of parenting.

I remember talking to a friend of mine who's a social worker in the Bronx and tends to middle school kids. I was pontificating on parenting culture today: how some Gen X parents are so hands-on they don't let their kids do anything for themselves, how they coddle their kids and micromanage their households.

"Uh, not where I am," she said. "I swear sometimes I think these parents had their kids just so they'd have someone to do errands for them. The kid gets home from school and it's like, 'Go get some milk,' and then they get home again and it's like, 'I forgot, we also need soda. Go back out.'" She's had to call social services several times because kids told her they were being beaten by their parents.

I can't imagine actually abusing my child, but I can imagine losing my temper. I have done that thing of picking Oliver up a little too tightly, putting him down in his crib a little too gruffly, when he's disobeying and I'm at my wits' end.

I know someone who in a fury closed the refrigerator door on his son because the boy wouldn't get out of the fridge after being told a million times to do so. He didn't really get hurt at all, but he could have. It's really scary. When you come out of the rage-fog, you think, *Oh my God, I could have done something awful.* Or, I suppose, some people think, *Oh my God, I just did something awful*. More than one in one hundred kids are victims of actual child abuse.[7]

This is worth fearing: neglect, physical and emotional abuse, cruelty. No child should be subjected to any of these things, ever. We should all do our part not to do this stuff to our kids, and to report abuse when we see it, or to help prevent it if we ever have the chance.

One friend of mine, a mother of three, saw another mother losing it with her child at the airport. She was screaming at the kid, getting rough. My friend, a saintlike woman, went over to the mother and instead of yelling at her for the way she was treating her child, said, "You look like you could use a break. Can I watch your son while you go get a cup of coffee?"

The mother, shocked, gratefully said yes. She went off and was gone for a while, so long that my friend started to wonder if she was being given this child to adopt. But no, there she was, the mother coming back. She'd washed her face, put her hair back, gotten a cup of coffee and a snack, and seemed like a whole different person. "Thank you," she said to my friend, and took her child's hand, much more calmly this time.

That's not to say she's never going to hit her kid now, or that you should always step in like that, but when it comes to abuse, which gets worse in hard economic times, everyone who's not part of this horrible problem should feel proud of themselves, and should do whatever they can to help kids and parents get out of the cycle.

The Hard Parts

Once I heard a sermon about a woman who'd had a terrible childhood. When she was a little girl, her family's home burned up before their eyes. That was bad, but what her mother said in that moment was worse: "Oh no! We lost everything! Everything! How will we ever recover? What's to become of us?"

Looking back, the woman wondered what life would have been like if, instead of falling apart, her mother had turned to her and her siblings and said, "Thank God you're safe. Thank God we all made it out of the house. This was scary, but everything is going to be okay. We have each other and somehow we'll get back on our feet. I'm just so grateful to have you with me."

The woman wished her mother had been stronger for her, yes, but she also wished she'd been made to see the far greater value of loved ones over things, and been encouraged to believe in the power of love and faith. Instead, she grew up afraid and bitter, and her mother never got over her doomsaying, even after they found a new home and new possessions. They were always just about to lose everything again. They were always afraid.

Of course there are catastrophes that are hard to recover from. It's not like you have to put a sunny face on every horror in order to be a good parent. This isn't about denial; it's about coping and not putting the burden of your adult problems off on your child. We owe it to our kids to make sure they feel safe and loved. We have an obligation to them to do whatever we need to do to have a sense of humor and to rally our brainpower toward finding solutions.

I often think about that sermon's wailing mother and how a slightly different attitude would have saved her children years of therapy. There's a lesson there for all of us day-to-day. Most of us don't have to deal with the sudden loss of everything we own the way that mother did, but we all have to deal with crises large and small that feel absolutely insurmountable. I like to refer to them as short trips to hell.

Here's an example: One day a couple of winters ago, my stepson, Blake, was in town and we decided to take him ice-skating at a park in Manhattan. Oliver was a few months old. He started to fuss on the very long line outside and there was no place in sight to nurse him comfortably. It was freezing and there was no place to sit. I soothed and rocked and told him we could find a bench once we got inside and he could nurse and I could get some hot cocoa and we could watch Blake and Daddy skate. I believed it myself. The end of the line offered warmth, nourishment, and peace.

Finally we got inside. It was mobbed and loud and still cold and you couldn't leave because there was no reentry.

By then Oliver was truly hungry, so I found a small spot on an icy metal bench by the lockers, reached through several layers, found a breast, and nursed him while teenagers bumped into my back and knees with their ice-skate blades. Neal took Blake off to skate. And as I sat there, holding on to all of our stuff, feeding my baby (not well—he kept arching his back in frustration), miserable and uncomfortable and cold and trying to figure out how I would make it through the next hour, I started crying. I felt trapped. There was no way out.

Yanking Neal and Blake off the ice and making them take an expensive taxi home didn't seem fair, especially when we'd waited on line so long. I knew Neal would relieve me if he could, but he didn't have his phone with him on the ice, and I was too far away to signal. Plus I would have to lug four people's bags over through the crowds to get to the ice and try to wave frantically to get him to see me. And I would have to do it with a baby on my breast, because Oliver was still nursing away, and apparently starving to death.

Then things got even worse: Oliver had a diaper blowout.

At this point I started laughing a little while I was crying. "Cocoa!" I thought out loud. "I actually believed I could have cocoa!"

I tried hard to piece together a plan that made sense: How could I ever get a diaper changed in a tiny stall on my lap in the chilly Port-a-Potty? How could I manage all our stuff with the baby to angle for help? How would I ever make it without water or a bathroom trip myself until we could go home? Would we ever get warm? And would they ever stop playing those blaring Christmas carols?

But as I sat there feeling sorry for myself, I realized Oliver was no longer trying to claw my shirt off. He'd calmed down and seemed actually content in spite of his diaper. So I bundled us back up and put all our stuff on my shoulders and put Oliver in his sling and headed out like some kind of Early Explorer to look for signs of friendly life. On the way to the ice rink, I passed a First Aid tent.

We were nowhere near frostbite. We had no injuries. We were just incredibly grumpy. Still, I took a risk and asked the gruff-looking man guarding the door if I could by any chance use the tent to change a diaper.

To my surprise, he smiled broadly, said his daughter was the same age, and ushered us in. Within, a heater hummed. It was warm and quiet. We were the only ones there. There were chairs and tables and a water fountain. I got a drink of water and changed Oliver's diaper, added another layer under his coat, nursed him a bit more leisurely this time, and got us all warmed up.

Within ten minutes, I felt like a new person. After profusely thanking the tent guard and cooing over his wallet photos, Oliver and I went out to the railing and watched Neal and Blake, who were having a wonderful time. Neal skated over and asked if I needed anything. "Yes, nachos!" I said. He went and got me some, plus a soda, and in that time I scored a seat. In the space of fifteen minutes, Oliver and I had gone from hungry, dirty, totally helpless, and miserable to totally happy and warm and comfortably seated and fed. I marveled at how fast things could turn from good to bad and back again.

When I talked to my friend Tara about this outing, she said I was brave to try to do so much with such a small baby, that this is why plenty of new parents opt not to leave the house at all—much less for complicated excursions to mid-Manhattan ice rinks.

"When your baby is upset and you have no immediate way to comfort him," she said, "it's basically like being in hell. I remember one time at the zoo with my father and all the kids in the family on a day that turned out to be a hundred and fifty degrees. We're at, like, the monkey exhibit, and the kids all have a simultaneous meltdown. So there we are with five young children covered in sweat and melted ice cream and snot and tears. And I turned to my dad and said, 'Look around you. This is the ninth circle of hell.'"

But she got out of there eventually, and commended me on having escaped my hell as well, and she concluded, "I guess the moral is: when you find yourself in hell, get out of hell."

I laughed, because it seemed kind of like tough love. Like, "When you find yourself depressed, get undepressed" (rather than, say, "Get Celexa, therapy, and a gym membership"). But there's no specific advice to give when each person's hell (and each week's or day's or month's hell) is so unique. But there's truth and comfort to be had from the advice "Get out of hell." It acknowledges the intensity of such moments, and it reminds you that escape is possible.

That's obvious when you're not in the moment, but when things have gone bad, it feels so final, like parenting is the most impossible thing ever and the agony of that crowded, freezing, cluttered skate cabin is never going to end. When, the fact is, in a certain time frame, you will be out of the meta-phorical skate cabin: the baby will eventually fall asleep, you will get your food, everyone will be consoled and nourished and achieve equilibrium again. And if you know that's what needs to happen, you can get very special-ops–style focused on taking steps in that direction.

There have been plenty of awful moments since then, and at every one I think, "Okay. Just get out of hell. There is a way out of hell."

It's not always a First Aid tent. Sometimes it's just bailing out and going home. Sometimes it's calling and canceling an appointment. Sometimes it's stepping into a McDonald's bathroom for a diaper change. Sometimes it's pulling off at the nearest exit and walking around at a gas station. Sometimes it's just taking it second by second and riding it out until hell transforms into purgatory. Nachos always help.

Party Time!

The day after Christmas, we were at the playground pushing our son around on his new tricycle from Santa, a Radio Flyer we'd put together the night before while watching *Christmas in July*. Oliver didn't know exactly what was going on, but he seemed very happy about the bike and the Christmas tree and the family being around. We were all aglow with our new presents and our excitement.

Oliver was playing with a little boy and we struck up a conversation with his parents and asked what they'd done for Christmas.

"Oh, he doesn't know the difference yet," the mother said of her toddler, "so we just got a sitter and went to the movies. We figure we don't have to do holidays or birthdays until he's at least three."

I almost choked on my deli coffee.

As if these things don't count unless the child will be able to recall it in detail. As if it's all for him, rather than also for you and your friends and his. As if celebrating is some kind of *burden*.

This reminds me of the trend toward casualness across the country: the funerals where people show up in sweats, the weddings where people show up in sneakers.

We have friends who are planning their wedding and say

they have never been to a good one. We spent a good long while recounting all the crazy, uncomfortable, and downright depressing weddings we've been to and then we recalled the very few that worked like magic, where when the wedding vows were read we couldn't help getting a chill down our backs.

All holidays and ceremonies, just like any kind of prayer or party, can be empty or full depending on who's doing the celebrating and the spirit of the event. When you have a kid, you're put in the position of officiant for the first time. You're no longer the person getting married or sitting in the pew; no longer the kid racing down the stairs to rip open packages. You're the priest; you're the host; you're *Santa.*

It's kind of terrifying, but also kind of awesome: Santa! You! (I know not everyone celebrates Christmas, but American that I am, I consider Santa totally without race, religion, or borders.)

And hosting is something I find incredibly fun. You have a bunch of people you like over and feed them and they all hang out and then they go home and you clean up and gossip about them. And when you have a party for a kid, you get to gossip about two generations of people! And you get to see your kid wired on sugar and maybe the most hyped up and giddy he will be until the next holiday or party!

And yet, people always find stuff to complain about. Want to know what I never thought people would have a problem with that they apparently do? Goodie bags. Apparently, those little bags kids get at the end of parties full of happy plastic toys is not just a friendly gesture and fun takeaway; it is a threat that must be stomped out.

In a "Family Life" column published by Reuters on May 5, 2008, Christopher Noxon set out guidelines for fixing the magic-free modern birthday party:

Step one: immediate and total ban on goodie bags. There was a time, not so long ago, when kids got genuinely excited by those little sacks of toys and do-dads that they routinely receive on their way out the door of a birthday party. That time is long gone. Now we've seen for ourselves the catalogs that sell kazoos and tattoos and superballs in bulk for less than a cent apiece. All these sad little bags do for us now is inspire worry about sweatshop labor and toxic plastic fumes.[8]

Noxon's not alone. Check out parenting message boards; they are full of similar calls to action against the goodie bag.

This is the same warped logic that causes parents to give out apples instead of Milky Way minis at Halloween. The fact is, on special occasions, more kids like plastic crap and chocolate bars with gooey centers than they do wholesome, organic, sugarless snacks and leaving empty-handed after downing a gluten-free cupcake and playing enriching word games.

The point of parties and holidays is they're special. They're a chance to step out of the workaday world in which you don't get free bouncy balls and kazoos and a plate full of frosting in the middle of the day.

Another supposedly wholesome trend is the "no gift" birthday party, which the *New York Times* described in a July 2007 article titled "Cake, but No Presents, Please":

In part to teach philanthropy and altruism, and in part as a defense against swarms of random plastic objects destined to clutter every square foot of their living space, a number of families are experimenting with gift-free birthday parties, suggesting that guests donate money or specified items to the charity of the child's choice instead.[9]

I don't know why I'm so violently turned off by the idea. It's not like I don't believe in giving to charities. I do it every year. But I guess I just love parties, and I love picking out gifts. I also love having presents around the house. Whenever Oliver reads the book *Toy Boat*, we talk about his friend Mars, who gave it to him. Whenever we play with his cool rubber cars, we think of his beloved "uncles" Kenny and Brendan, who gave them to him for his second birthday. Gifts are a constant reminder of the gifters.

I also really like that he's learning manners every time he gives or gets a present. It makes me crazy when kids rip open piles of presents with no notice of who's given them. I like when kids open a present, look it over, and go hug the giver and thank him. Maybe it's not exactly what they wanted, but they learn to express gratitude for everything.

I'm really glad that Miss Manners, whom I idolize, agrees with me on this front. She is pro–gift-parties, too, because of the opportunity to teach kids to be generous and polite.

Sure, maybe you can get that from charity parties, but on one's special day, there's something more appealing to me about giving and getting from people you know than introducing anonymous beneficiaries.

In an article I edited, the writer Amy S. F. Lutz wrote

Despite the old joke that "every day is children's day," birthdays are really the only day kids get to be the absolute center of attention, the only day that is all about what they (and not their siblings, friends or even the homeless or the cancer patients) want. Teaching them to be charitable, that's what we want. Lucky for us, we get the other 364 days. That's plenty of time.[10]

Hear, hear!

Of course, the materialistic extreme is just as bad.

In another article, "Birthdays Gone Wild!," Asra Q. Nomani wrote this:

> For my son's first birthday, I rented a newborn tiger cub from a local country zoo (cost: $200 for two hours). My lame justification: my son's name, Shibli, means "my lion cub," and, yes, I first asked for lion cubs. For his second birthday, I had custom-designed invitations ($42.20), rented a barn at a place called Rich Farm outside of town, and booked a hay ride and karaoke machine (final price tag: about $300). For his third birthday, I rented a white stretch limo ($300) and had the driver take us to a home recording studio ($275), where my son cut his first CD, belting out the "Dump Truck Song," with his own lyrics. It went something like this: "Dump truck! Dump truck! DUMP TRUCK! DUMP TRUCK!"[11]

The punch line of her story? The only party her five-year-old son remembers is the cheap one where she baked a lop-sided pirate ship cake.

It's obvious that those huge parties are not usually for the kids. I went to a birthday party for a three-year-old that had fifty guests, of which a good twenty or so were toddlers, packed into a craft studio. I certainly appreciated the wine. Oliver appreciated the balloon animals and to a lesser extent the organic T-shirts and fabric paint. We both enjoyed the pizza and the cupcakes. It was by all measures a high-quality party. And yet, it was also completely overwhelming. We went home and both took a three-hour nap.

When later that afternoon we ran into friends who had been at the party, we all seemed totally hung over. We'd probably consumed about three glasses of wine between the four of us. Still, it was like the morning after a raging kegger. Oliver and his friend and we parents all stood around at the playground in a daze. And we didn't feel warm fuzzy feelings of love and harmony. We just felt *exhausted*.

There's a pretty rich middle ground between the depleting monster-party and the antisocial bailout. The tips that I like are these: Keep it to two hours and give the start and stop times in the invite. Plan it around the most common nap times. Provide food and drink that both kids and adults will like—juice boxes and beer; mac 'n' cheese and . . . bread and cheese. Or something else hearty. I just like cheese.

A friend's wife who is something of an expert at birthday parties, having thrown three kids' worth, says it's essential to keep the party moving: "Parties work best when kids can be directed from one activity to the next," she says. "Okay, time to dance! Time for a potty break! Time to bash the piñata! Time for a teenager to show up dressed in a sweaty SpongeBob costume! Time to go outside! Time for cake! Here's your goody bag. What's your hurry?"

My friend says, "I remember being surprised at one of our first birthday parties we threw how many different activities my wife had scheduled and she said something like, 'What did you think they'd do—sit around drinking wine and eating hummus and talking about real estate?'"

Some people say to keep the number of guests to your child's age plus one—like if your kid is four you have five child guests. That seems a little harsh to me, and I reserve the right to invite all our favorite friends (who, luckily, are so far Oliver's favorite "aunts" and "uncles," too). Neal likes to make a signature cocktail, like a lime rickey or a mojito, and to call it an Oliver-tini. And yes, festive cocktailing gets people sloppy fast, but they can't get *that* drunk in a two-hour span, especially when they're eating lots of cheese. And even a couple of martinis won't make adults as nuts as the kids will get after a big slice of chocolate cake. So you can all get crazy together and all sleep very well that night.

Illness

I asked a daycare teacher I know how her job was going.

Not well, it turned out. "Parents drop off their sick babies," she said. "They dose them with Tylenol and leave them with us. Then the fever spikes up again a couple hours later. These poor babies, hot and coughing and just wanting to be held all day." She called one of the sick kid's parents and he didn't come to get the kid until two and a half hours later. A months-old baby!

You don't want to be judgmental about other parents if you can help it, and Lord knows there but for the grace of God go I. Who knows what they're going through, what their work demands are, what's on their plate? When I worked at a daycare center in Texas, I felt sorry for the families who had their kids in that windowless place eleven hours a day, even on holidays. They were clearly working crazy long hours and still couldn't afford anything better than that low-rent facility. (It paid so badly that the staff turnover was nearly constant. One day the kids in the twos room woke up from their nap to find that their beloved lead teacher had quit and been replaced. All the potty-trained kids regressed.)

Anyway, you hate to think how bad things must be for that to be the best you can do for your kids. I get very sad thinking about sick babies missing their parents. The teacher I knew wasn't sad; she was angry. These parents were putting her and the babies at risk of getting sick and keeping the whole class in a constant state of passed-around illness. Another teacher I spoke to said, "It's not just depressing; it's illegal! The Department of Health forbids sick kids from coming to school." I don't think it's a coincidence that the school eventually wound up with a scarlet fever epidemic.

When Oliver had a 104-degree fever one day when he was two, all he wanted to do was cuddle. I felt so sorry for him, but it was also amazing to be such a source of comfort. As long as he was attached to my body, he was comfortable, able to sleep and relatively happy. Joined that way, we sipped juice, watched old movies, and snuggled in bed. It was as if he were a baby again, with all the good and bad that go along with having a totally dependent infant.

Other sicknesses haven't been so warm and soft and comfortable. The last cold came on at midnight one night, a high fever and a runny nose. And even Tylenol, juice, and cuddling couldn't make him happy. He was just furious, and spent the next two days fussing and lashing out. He woke up every two hours at night. During the day, he burst into tears whenever faced with the slightest irritation (running out of noodles in his soup, not being able to get through a doorway with an open umbrella, not being able to finish an ABC puzzle).

I was so sorry for him, and so exasperated. Because of course I was sick by then, too, and as we know, it's way harder to take care of others when we feel lousy. I didn't totally lose it, but I did at one point in frustration throw a container of baby powder across the room. Public Service Announcement: if you are annoyed and need to throw something, go get a bath toy.

This way you will not leave a residue of cornstarch over every surface in your bedroom.

Within forty-eight hours it was all over. Everyone was back on his feet. *Snow White* had been watched fourteen times. Gallons of apple juice and strawberry milk had been consumed. Except for the video rental late fees and garbage bags full of Kleenex, it was like it had never happened.

So many kids we know are sick constantly. And it seems like parents of our generation trust The Google over their pediatricians or even their own instincts.

Author Kim Brooks, the mother of one such kid, wrote

Like most parents of "basically healthy" kids, I had been operating under the assumption that when it came to medical treatments and interventions, assuming the illness was not putting the baby at any grave or long-term risk, less was more. . . . That was what I thought for seven long months during which he endured half-a-dozen ear infections and at least as many colds, acid reflux and RSV, and two separate cases of the Rotavirus. But at some point along the way, I simply realized that "wait and see" wasn't working. I decided that modern medicine, with all of its potential side effects and scary unknowns, was going to be my son's new best friend.[12]

She wound up going to a bunch of specialists and getting her son well, genuinely well. Her fear of the medical establishment was overcome.

I've been a big fan of modern medicine since my appendix burst and doctors saved my life.

I love nurses even more, and not just because that's what my lovely in-laws did for a living.

I mean, how great is the Poison Help Hotline (800-222-1222)? I've called it just once to date, when Oliver wandered into the bathroom when he was about one year old, found a tube of toothpaste on the floor, and gobbled some. I was making dinner and he'd been playing on the floor next to me, so it took me just a minute to get to him, but he'd already managed to smear his whole mouth with the stuff. I called the hotline, got a good education in fluoride, and was reassured that he would be okay. I also got way more hardcore about keeping anything toxic off the floor.

But what I really got was a further appreciation that there are experts out there who know a hell of a lot more than I do about my child's health. And given that I just eked out those college science requirements, that sure is a relief.

What We Talk About When We Talk About Our Kids

It's interesting how after the age of five, kids are photographed way less, blogged about way less, and generally discussed nowhere near as much. There are many explanations for this:

Freaked out parents have gotten it under control by then and aren't as desperate for information and reassurance.

Kids aren't cute in the same crazy, huge-eyed alien-esque way.

Ecstatic parents aren't quite as hypnotized and shocked by the sight of their tween as they were by their newborn.

After the age of two you don't have the constant milestones of first words, first steps, first day of school, and so on.

But I think part of why we lose a bit of interest in documenting older kids is that they're no longer extensions of their parents in the same way, and we're not usually spending as much time with them each day.

Babies are dependent, needy and, conveniently for some, don't typically have the force of personality and expression that they will have later in life. Their range of needs is limited and they sleep a lot (although not always at the most desirable times). And they don't really know what's going on. This makes it very easy to project onto them complex emotions, nefarious or angelic motives, and intricate identities that may or may not have any basis in reality. (See above references to the wonder that is my baby.)

I'm always shocked by those e-mail addresses or license plates like EmmasMom@gmail.com or MOMMY24. Of course, it can feel like the ground has shifted under your feet when you become a parent. Suddenly someone else is more important than you. As the saying goes, it's like walking around for the rest of your life with your heart outside your chest.

But parenthood doesn't obliterate all that went before. It doesn't replace the rest of your life. People have been having kids for a long time. It doesn't have to annihilate everything else in your life: time, money, career, sex, relationships with your partner and your friends.

Neal has always been really adamant about not ever making Oliver an excuse. If we don't go to a party, it's not because we couldn't get a babysitter; it's because we aren't up to it or because we have other plans. When people say they can't make a deadline because of their kid, I always silently scoff, because I have a kid, too, and I still make deadlines. If I screw up, it's my fault, not parenthood's. Blaming innocent little kids for your own flaws or failings seems awfully low.

We all know people who talk only about their kids. They're really boring. It's like going on and on about a movie no one else has seen. And of course we're all super in love with and proud of our kids, so it is a struggle to not talk about them constantly, but find other things to talk about we must.

We can't let our identity get totally bound up in our kids. Not only is it boring, but also, the kids aren't going to be little forever. We're cruising for a major crash when they leave for college. The empty nest will seem a lot emptier if we don't have anything else but kids in our lives. And there we'll be checking our AARP e-mails at FelixsMama@hotmail.com.

Having Faith

When I was three or so, my parents tried to read me Bible stories. As soon as I heard about Jesus's side being pierced and him crying out for his father on the cross, I burst into tears and shrieked, "Too scary!"

My parents figured they'd given it a shot, and so never mentioned it again.

"Couldn't you have started with the parables or something?" I asked them years later when I was studying religion in college and feeling like I wished I could have had some personal frame of reference for all the church history and theology I was learning. Instead it was like a fascinating foreign language, one I would probably never master and would certainly never have the right accent for. Whatever the equivalent to rolling your r's is in matters of faith, I didn't have it.

But then, when Neal and I were doing premarital counseling, we started meeting with the priest who would marry us, and I just sort of got it. It made sense to me why people had religion in their life, how belief and nonbelief were on a spectrum, and that you could participate in the whole God-worshipping thing without sacrificing a belief in science, in reason, or in, say, the Catholic Church's being deeply troubled.

I made sure to get Oliver baptized. I wanted to get some godparents for him, and I wanted to get a church's blessing on him, and I wanted to thank the Almighty for such a ridiculously lovely son. They let you pick three godparents in the Episcopal Church. We put down my best friend, Tara; Neal's best friend, Michelle; and my cousin Rhoades (plus, understood, his wife, Hannah). So Oliver has four godparents, who not only are responsible for his religious life, whatever that winds up being like, but they're also there to look after him if anything happened to us. They stood up before God, renounced the Devil (that really is part of the ceremony!), and said they would be there for him. That makes me sleep a little better at night.

Oliver loves Disney movies. Part of it is because it gives him something to talk about with the girls on the playground and with his favorite cousin, Harper, but also I think because he enjoys the stories and likes the idea of protectors appearing to take care of people in distress. "You're my fairy godmother!" he told Tara one day when she stopped by for coffee and gave him a book. "That's right," she said, smiling.

When Tara's daughter, who goes to Catholic school, was confirmed, I found out about this amazing tradition called the palanca letter. The confirmation candidate goes on a retreat with the others in her confirmation group and at some point in the weekend, she is handed a bag of letters from friends and family. She doesn't know in advance that she's going to get them. They just are dropped in her lap and she's given some time alone to read through them.

In my letter, I told her I thought it was so important to have a spiritual life. You get things from religion you don't get from anywhere else. Feeling a connection to something greater provides a kind of comfort and solace that even a best friend or a sibling or a parent can't.

Atheism is popular these days, as are some rather terrifying branches of evangelicalism, and there's something about both schools that makes me a little anxious. I guess it's just that they both seem so *sure*, and my relationship to God and death has very little conviction to it. Mostly I'm just all faith and curiosity and gratitude. I know a lot of people who pride themselves on being too smart for religion, but how can you have a child, a process at once so mundane and so mind-blowing, and maintain that level of hubris?

In the classic parenting book *The Blessing of a Skinned Knee*, the author, Wendy Mogel, writes that when she worked as a child psychiatrist, she used to find herself facing parents who wanted a diagnosis and a medication when she kept wanting to say that the problem wasn't biological, it was spiritual. A lot of the kids who were brought to her didn't have ADD or anything like that; they needed moral guidance and they weren't getting it. Their problem wasn't a deficit of attention; it was a deficit of character. And it turns out that's not a problem with a quick pharmaceutical fix.

Community, whether you get it from a church or a school or a neighborhood or somewhere else, is so important. Until I became a parent, I didn't feel nearly as invested in politics, in my community, or in world affairs. I followed the news. I voted. I believed in being a decent citizen. I glared at people who littered. I did a little volunteering.

But having a child made me so much more aware of how much we need one another. I need companionship when I have Oliver for the whole day alone. I need the other parents on the playground to make small talk with. I need the neighbors to say hi to us and hold the door for our stroller. I need our babysitter, and my mother, and Oliver's school.

Need is a strong word. Without these people and institutions, I would get by, I'm sure. I would find something to do all day. We'd do swim classes or something. But an organic social fabric is really something special. It holds you up all day—breaks up the monotony, gives you an outlet, let's your child feel like he's not just alone with you for endless stretches of time on a desert island inhabited by string cheese and Melissa & Doug puzzles.

In *The Parents We Mean to Be: How Well-Intentioned Adults Undermine Children's Moral and Emotional Development*, Richard Weissbourd writes, "Children need adults who require them to be helpful, whether it's caring for a younger sibling, getting groceries for a neighbor, or performing routine household chores. Requiring children to be helpful not only builds caring skills but makes attending to others reflexive."[13]

It's good for our neighbors, good for us, and, it turns out, necessary for our kids, to make them take out the trash, and to encourage them to believe in something greater than themselves.

In Praise of Stepchildren

Whenever anyone points at our stroller and asks, "Oh, is he your first baby?" there's an awkward moment. Usually, I'll just say, "Yes," which is technically true. I've only ever been pregnant once. But if it's someone my husband and I expect to talk to for longer than it takes to get through the grocery checkout line, I'll usually say, "Actually, he [pointing at my seven-month-old son] has a thirteen-year-old brother from his [pointing at my husband] first marriage." People usually then ask how old my husband is (thirty-one) and then try to determine if he's a deadbeat dad or a hero.

Of course, he's neither. He's just, to his first child, a loving but noncustodial parent with all that goes with the title: weekly phone calls, monthly child-support payments, seasonal visits. My stepson, Blake, who is adorable and brilliant and immense fun to have around, lives most of the year with his mother in Texas. We fly him up for a few weeks of the summer and a couple of weeks at Christmas, and we go, or just my husband goes, down to Texas a couple of times a year for a few days at a time. It's not nearly enough, but we take what we can get.

The memoirist Rebecca Walker once wrote that parents love their biological kids more than their nonbiological kids.[14] The blogosphere erupted.

I don't understand why anyone would say she loved one kid, or one parent, more than another, even under duress. Then again, I'm plunged into a crisis of conscience every time someone asks to be my Facebook friend, so maybe I'm not the best judge of what's too difficult a loyalty question.

Personally, I love being a stepmother. What a luxury to have a big kid just plunked down in your life like that. And how lucky my baby is to have such a cool big brother. It's awkward to have to launch into an explanation when someone asks if Oliver is an only child, but a little awkwardness is a small price to pay for the gift of a bigger family.

Separation Anxiety

Some days when I drop off Oliver at nursery school, he couldn't care less that I'm leaving. I have to chase him down to get him to say "Bye" before he's totally immersed himself in bean shakers and Play-Doh. Other days, he clings to me like the floor is made of hot lava.

After cuddling and talking encouragingly for ten minutes, I have a teacher help me pry him off and she takes him to the window to wave good-bye to me on the other side. Sometimes he waves happily. Sometimes he wails and the last thing I see before I go to work is my son's face contorted in misery. Even though I know from the teachers' report that he "is wriggling to get out of Miss Rachel's arms and go play the second the curtain closes," that image is haunting.

It doesn't help that for the past two months straight he's cried whenever anyone but me picked him up from school. The teacher says, "Open ears and sneaky feet!" And then, "Oliver, come walking!" And around the corner he comes. If it's me, he smiles and runs happily to hug me. If it's Neal or his grandmother or his babysitter Erica, he runs back to Miss Rachel crying. He loves all these people. They are not abusive. They are just not his mother, and right now he's into me.

You'd think this would be flattering: to be the center of someone's life. And yet, it's really a lot of pressure. It doesn't make me feel good that Neal gets the shaft when he's just as hands-on. It's particularly unjust what Oliver puts Neal through at school because the second they're out on the sidewalk, he's chatting away and the two of them have a wonderful lunch and playtime.

Neal all but says, "Could you please go back into the school lobby and tell the other parents that I'm not in fact the monster you just made me seem like?"

We know these things are phases. In a year, he'll be super into Neal. Still, the gesture feels like a repudiation of our equal parenting and it hurts Neal's feelings. It also makes me feel guilty for not being there.

I try to teach Oliver to say, "Yay, Daddy!" when he sees Neal. He doesn't go for it.

I start to wonder if Neal isn't the problem in some way. But no, he's a good father, affectionate and fun. They have a good time.

I start to wonder if maybe I'm just incredibly awesome, if I would be sad if I weren't around if I were my kid. But no, I am not a superior parent. I get grouchy and lame out sometimes on getting gumballs from the gumball machine by lying and saying I don't have any quarters.

Miss Rachel says she's not worried about it, that kids just get in habits only tangentially related to their actual feelings. She said some kids just get hooked on doing something extreme like that. Like, for weeks Dylan E. would yell, "NOOOOOOOOOOO!" as soon as circle time started. Another kid runs into the threes classroom when it's time for pickup. This is just Oliver's thing right now, and it's not fun for anyone, but eventually he'll grow out of it or replace it with something else.

But then Neal leaves town for a couple of weeks and Oliver can't stop talking about Daddy and how much he misses him. He even goes up to strange men on the playground and tries to get them to play ball with him or talk to him. He's actually gotten me into a couple of fun conversations this way. If I were a single mom, he would be a good wingman (uh, wing-toddler).

And then, just like that, the phase is over. When other people pick him up, he smiles happily. He runs out and hugs Neal. And it's like all those months of rejection never happened.

Regretting Your Life

"If I'd known then what I know now, I never would have had kids," a mother I know once told me. "Sometimes I just want to get in my car and drive away and never come back. The guilt is unbearable."

I was single at the time and wondered if this was common among people with kids. But when I told another friend she was aghast: "That's horrible! If I'd known then what I know now, I might have married someone different, but I would never give back my children. They're my life. I love them more than anything in the world. How could a life without them compare?"

Now that I have a child of my own, I'm on the second friend's side. It's good to have a fantasy life for yourself, but you have to realize it's not real. And getting nostalgic about a former life is deadly. I knew the first mom when she was single and childless, and the fact is, her life wasn't that great. I want to ask her, what did she think she'd become? And why can't she become that now?

People love to talk about when they were young and beautiful. A friend of mine likes to respond, "You were *young* . . ."

That's how I feel when people start talking about how awesome their life was when they were young and hip and childless: "You were *young and childless* . . ."

Some people think that going to adult-kid shows where they can drink beer while their kids dance around to rock music will preserve their membership in the hip club.

But those events aren't cool. They have an air of desperation about them, those Velvet Underground onesies and all-ages shows, the parents trying to find bands they can agree on with their kids, their desire to maintain certain cultural standards in their homes. "My kid only listens to Sonic Youth," a proud father will say. "Everything except *Daydream Nation.*"

Doing this just trains your kids to adjust their tastes to please you, and sets them up to become huge fans of polka when they rebel as teenagers.

And there's no need to fight so hard to hold on to some idea of yourself as formerly-and-perhaps-still cool.

Getting out of the house does become a bit more complicated once you have kids. There's more to do. You may not always sleep as much as you would if you didn't have children to take care of. But to turn your kid into an excuse for why you can't make it to a party or meet a deadline or go to your friends' place for a visit seems like the height of copping out.

That's why those "Baby on Board" signs are so stupid. As if everyone around you is supposed to drive differently just because you have a child on board? As if they will see the sign and think, *Ah! I was going to crash into that car for sport, but now will not!*

My writer friends have a ton of kids and jobs between them and they're never late on stories. So when I get a whiny e-mail about how a kid got the sniffles and therefore it was impossible to do xyz, I think, *my friends would have done it.* Lots of parents throughout the ages have somehow managed to live their lives and enjoy their children.

Plenty of things get harder, but so much else gets so much better. And every family is different. How pleasurable or hard it will be depends on your disposition, your relationship, your career, your friends, what kind of baby you get, and a million other factors, including whether or not there are twenty-four-hour drugstores and good takeout in your area.

The sleep thing was a little tricky in the first months. Cleaning the apartment rather than going to bed early always wound up being a mistake. But we came up with a plan: stay in bed twelve hours a day and we're sure to get seven of sleep. Oliver was in a little crib next to us. All three of us were in the bed area from nine p.m. to nine a.m. Sometimes we watched old movies. (Turns out babies are partial to black and white and red, so they get really into classic films, especially anything with dancing, like Fred and Ginger's *Swing Time*. Oh, and *2001: A Space Odyssey* blew that child's *mind*.)

More often, we lounged. The baby nursed. We read magazines, napped, or chatted. We marveled at how superior Oliver was to all other babies.

Contrary to all the naysayers, during those first months I got more sleep, had more sex, and had more time on my hands than I'd had since my midtwenties.

And then a few months later when Neal had to go on tour and I was alone with the baby for a week, all hell broke loose at work and I developed a stress stomachache and a cold. The whole thing seemed way too difficult. *How does anyone ever work and have kids?* I wondered. *How does anyone ever do anything and have kids?*

But I dragged myself to work each day and put out fires. I had my mother come over and bring food. It all worked out fine, ultimately, although now I make sure to line up lots of extra help on those days when Neal's out of town.

The moral is, you never know when or how you're going to be overwhelmed, so there's no use psyching yourself up for a hard time.

When I interviewed Supernanny (also known as Jo Frost) for the *New York Times* a few years ago, she turned the tables and asked if I had kids. I told her not yet, but that my husband and I were talking about it. "Good for you!" she said, praising us for discussing it in advance. She said so many of the families she counseled had just had the kids without talking about how they wanted to raise them or why they wanted them in the first place. She said, and I agree, that the more you discuss things in advance, the easier they are when they finally get there, as long as the discussions are constructive rather than anxiety producing.

When I was pregnant, I e-mailed the writer Shalom Auslander to thank him for an essay he'd written about the Lucy Cousins book character Maisy the mouse. He'd written hilariously about hating those books, and the essay included this passage: "Friends, social life, sex, money, time; I anticipated difficulties with all these things before our son was born. What I hadn't anticipated was his complete lack of skepticism."

Specifically, the only problem Shalom finds is that his son loves the simple-minded, hyper-enthusiastic, totally guileless children's book character Maisy Mouse, turning story time into an internal struggle between what he wants to say about these books and how he wants to keep from spoiling his son's naïve devotion to them.

It's so smart what he says, because it's true that you can't at all anticipate where challenges will come from, and because scapegoating your kid for your lack of time or sex or money is so unfair to them and to yourself. It is possible to have a fulfilling life, of which your kid is a part. To tell yourself that it's impossible to have both a baby and a job and friends is just lame.

Shalom wrote me back and said, "Did you ever realize that all your friends who are boring since they've had kids were pretty boring before they had kids?"

And it's true: some of our most miserable, harried friends act like they have a long list of fabulous parties they would be attending, novels they would be writing, and millions they would be making, if only they didn't have a baby around—when in fact they'd just be staying home watching sitcom reruns even if they were still child-free.

If anything, our life has become so much richer in the last two years. We've made a ton of new friends and gotten so much closer to some of our old friends. Who knew my husband's show-biz colleagues were so ready to become "aunts" and "uncles"?

Inevitably, you lose a few prebaby friends, especially anyone too babylike themselves. There's only room for one demanding person in your life, and the baby is much cuter than your drunken former coworker.

My friend Lisa said for her the first year of motherhood was hell, but then it was like having "the world's best roommate."

Oliver's good friend's parents say their only real problem has been finding childcare they can afford. And yet, they've cobbled together help from a bunch of different sources, including the women who run the store on their block and shower the little boy with love.

Every problem has a solution. They're not all silver bullets. Plenty have unwanted side effects. Guilt may be attached to some or most of them. But there's no excuse for blaming your kid for ruining your fabulous prebaby life.

Be honest: it wasn't that great.

Vaccination Paranoia

The '60s made us believe that all authority is bad. We've internalized that sensibility such that we mistrust everyone in a position of power, regardless of whether or not they're in that position for a reason. The irony is that now we tend to trust people not in power: a random poster on some message board, another parent at the park, or an article in a fringe magazine. The scientific method doesn't have the same emotional pull as a weeping mother on *Oprah*. If that mother is convinced that her child's illness was caused by a cooking spray, good luck proving to others that she is wrong, even with a million flawless control studies.

There's a difference, though, between being an authority and being *authoritarian*. We can accept the help of authorities when they're not authoritarian. Doctors should get better at explaining things to patients in their own terms, but we should also get better at trusting that not every decision made by someone in a position of power is a conspiracy.

Having studied science, and realizing how absolutely non-intuitive so much of it is, my first thought is that instinct must be utterly abandoned when it comes to anything medical. In the case of statistics, you must under no circumstances trust your instincts, for they are invariably wrong. I was flabbergasted by the famous "Birthday Problem," which says that there's more than a 50 percent chance of two people in a group of twenty-three having the same birthday. I would have guessed you'd need a class of at least a hundred.

And that's why I didn't become a statistician.

But one pediatrician I spoke with said parents should still use their instincts when it comes to medical issues. They just need to recognize that their own knowledge isn't enough in every circumstance, and that they need to consult with people who know more than they do for help with their decision. "My job as a pediatrician is to convince people they know what they're doing," said this doctor. That means explaining why vaccinations are necessary and separating out the myths from the facts about immunization.

But that's not enough for a startling number of parents.

Some aren't vaccinating because they don't have proper access to medical care.

Others aren't vaccinating because they have convinced themselves, or been convinced by irresponsible news reports and celebrity spokespeople, that there is some danger inherent in routine vaccination, that autism is caused by vaccines and can be cured by all manner of kooky techniques.

Dr. Paul Offit, author of *Autism's False Prophets* and coin-ventor of the rotavirus vaccine, suggests that the current crop of autism cures say, in effect, " 'Get off your ass as a mother and stop sitting around and whining about this and do something to help your child.' Give them antifungal medicines, give them antiviral medicines, give them gluten-free or casein-free diets, and your child will be better."[15]

And then when the child doesn't improve, it's the mother's fault, not the crackpot treatment's. Dr. Offit has devoted his career to not giving families of autistic children false hope, and also to showing that the fears surrounding vaccines are unfounded.

"When I stand up for vaccine science or vaccine safety," Dr. Offit says, "I do it because I care about the little guy. Because I care about the child in Minnesota whose parent chooses not to give them a vaccine and then watches the child die from meningitis. Or the parents in San Diego who choose not to give their children the measles vaccine and then watch their children get hospitalized with severe dehydration from measles. There's a lot of misinformation out there that gets put out in the name of standing up for the little guy but then it does exactly the opposite."

"Oh yeah, Dr. Profit," a woman I spoke to at a conference scoffed when I said I'd enjoyed *Autism's False Prophets*. "As if people who don't vaccinate put other people at risk."

"But you do," I said, suddenly really mad at her, both for dismissing the entirety of the scientific findings and for by all reputable accounts putting my son at risk for diseases he's been vaccinated against.

"There was an outbreak of measles in the Netherlands in 1999–2000," Dr. Offit says. "It was big, and it involved about four thousand children. What's interesting is that you were less likely to get measles if you were completely unvaccinated living in a highly vaccinated community than if you were completely vaccinated living in a relatively unvaccinated community. Which is to say that if you're in a school or an environment where other kids aren't vaccinated then you're at risk. No vaccine is one hundred percent effective and if you're not living in a herd that's immune, then you're at risk."

I am a firm believer in science and on following concrete evidence when it comes to things like vaccination. We have an instinctive desire to protect our children, and if we listen to our instincts, we know that the best way to protect them is to trust the people who truly understand the workings of illness: doctors, not celebrities or pundits with agendas.

Neal and I do pretty much everything our pediatrician tells us to, which has included sleep-training, getting rid of the bottle by the time Oliver was two (although—shhhh!—we have been lax about graduating from the sippy cup), and eating dinner together every night as a family. We can tell he wants what's best for our child, just like we do, and that he has no goal other than our child growing up happy and healthy and on track to reach his full potential.

Likewise, it's worth listening to the AAP on what kinds of illnesses to immunize against. Unless we all want to go to medical school, we should maybe let them figure shot schedules out for us.

The Great Circumcision Debate

If you want to have a really weird conversation, ask a parent if she circumcised her son.

Since the AAP restated in 2005 that circumcision was not medically necessary and so was mainly done for cosmetic or cultural reasons, the question of whether or not to have the procedure done has become one of the most hotly contended of all parenting questions.[16]

Online groups have compared it to female genital mutilation. Families have been torn asunder by a couple's choice to break from tradition, one way or the other. One blogger, Cole Gamble, provided a tongue-in-cheek summary of the classic "Will Make Son Look More Like Daddy" pro-circumcision argument: "Assuming daddy is foreskin-less as well, their similarity, anatomically speaking, is something they can bond over, like when they play catch."[17]

The AAP is in fact very easygoing about it all: "Existing scientific evidence demonstrates potential medical benefits of newborn male circumcision; however, these data are not sufficient to recommend routine neonatal circumcision. In circumstances in which there are potential benefits and risks, yet the procedure is not essential to the child's current well-being, parents should determine what is in the best interest of the child."

But what does "best interest" mean?

People have really strong feelings about that. When Neal and I were in the course of making that decision for Oliver, I asked around and got a million different responses, none of them comforting or definitive.

Hippie childbirth-class teacher [*equivocating*]: "I guess I lean toward not doing it, but my husband really wanted to, so my son is circumcised."

Midwife [*businesslike*]: "Is your husband circumcised?" Me: "Yes, and everyone else in our families." Her: "What does he say?" Me: "I guess he thinks maybe we should because he and my stepson and everyone in the family are?" Her: "Well, then maybe you should."

Circumcising nurse [*bored*]: "I have to read you this release that states you realize there's no medical reason for doing this." Me [*suddenly wondering if we've made the wrong choice*]: "Uh, yes?" Her: "Okay, hand me the baby."

Head of Labor and Delivery at hospital [*conspiratorial*]: "They did a great job! It's perfect. They didn't take off too much or too little. He'll be very happy when he's older!"

European nurse at the hospital upon changing a diaper right before we left the hospital [*appalled*]: "Oh no, you circumcised! *Tsk-tsk.* In my country, we consider this barbaric."

It's enough to make a person crazy. Not doing it, you may be in for less of the negative stuff, but I don't think so. People I know who didn't do it also say they've faced raised eyebrows and judgment. As in so many seemingly simple choices, there's no winning these days.

The only comment I really treasured was our pediatrician's: "I'm neutral on the subject. It doesn't matter one way or the other. Just pick and then never think about it again." That's easier said than done, but an admirable goal.

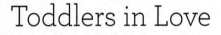

Toddlers in Love

Every March since three years ago, when I reported a story on baseball groupies at spring training, we've returned to Port Saint Lucie, Florida, to watch the Mets and to get some sun. It's a cheap flight, cheap hotel, and baseball game tickets are only about $10. It's always about seventy-eight degrees. Also, the Treasure Coast is made for old people, and it turns out old people and toddlers have a lot of the same passions: naps, handicap-access walkways, and five p.m. dinnertimes. This makes even dingy little coastal towns paradise for parents of young kids.

This past year when we went, Oliver was missing his nursery school friends and desperate to hang out with other kids. So when at a game a little girl about seven years old sat down in the aisle at the end of our row, right by the field, he immediately ran down there and sat next to her. He opened with his standard: "I'm Oliver! I'm two!"

Without taking her eye off the field, she said hi and started explaining how she was going to get a ball from the players. He soaked it all up and then asked her name. "Sierra," she said. He didn't quite get it. "What's your name?" he repeated. She patiently said, "My little brother couldn't say it either until he was like three. It's *Sierra*."

In between lessons in the finer points of baseball, Oliver

asked her name a few more times. Finally she said, "I've told you a million times! Sierra! Sierra-Sierra-Sierra-Sierra-Sierra!" She wasn't angry, just exasperated. He paused for a second to process her tirade and then looked up at her and said, happily, "Oh, I see."

Meantime, she'd signaled to a ballplayer and he'd given her the thumbs-up. When he went back to the dugout, he tossed her a ball. She stared at it in rapture and then ran back to her mother holding it in the air. Oliver stared after her as if she were a goddess. He started running up the stairs.

"Where are you going?" I asked him.

"Sierra!" he said, as if it were a stupid question.

He has a crush on her, I thought, and then I immediately felt embarrassed. That was a bit of a grown-up projection. Can't a kid befriend a person of the opposite sex without suddenly having a little "boyfriend" or "girlfriend"?

Miriam Axel-Lute, a writer I know from Albany, New York, went through the same thing with her kid. She wrote

> *Before I had a toddler, I often felt like there was a deep collective yearning out there to return to the age of arranged marriages. How else could I explain it, this drive to constantly see adult relationships and motivations in the most innocent of childhood social development? . . . I was certainly not going to indulge in inventing a love life for any prepubescent kid of mine, let alone one who was still in diapers.*[18]

But of course she totally wound up indulging in it, and so did I.

I mean, I didn't bust out the wedding cake, but I had trouble seeing Oliver's feelings for Sierra as anything but a protocrush.

Plus, Sierra was really nice. She seemed to genuinely find him charming. She opened his horizons and taught him about the world of baseball spring training. This seemed like a great formative romantic experience. "He's going to be happy in love," I found myself predicting, with some measure of self-congratulation. "It's because he's so loving and secure."

This surety about his future romantic happiness lasted about twenty-four hours. The next day, Oliver tried the same trick at the rental car place with a girl lounging in the chair opposite him. "I'm Oliver! I'm two!" he opened.

She glared at him, then shifted in her chair so she was facing the other way. He walked around to the other side and said, smiling, "Hi!"

She sighed heavily, climbed off the chair, and stomped off to her mother, where she complained that she was being "bothered."

This seemed like a less great formative romantic experience. But I was encouraged that he just shrugged and walked back to me, like, *her loss*. It kills me to think of him getting his heart broken. And I seethe at kids who don't respond warmly to his overtures of friendship. But both experiences are good preparation for life, and that's what he's in the business of: getting to know the world the way it is, in all its Sierra-loveliness and pink-shirt-girl-obnoxiousness.

After she showed the ball off to her mother, Sierra came back and sat with Oliver for the rest of the game. All the boys in the section, having witnessed Sierra's success, had flocked to that railing, so now standing next to Sierra and Oliver were about six boys in mitts angling for the next foul ball. But the two talked to each other as if they were all alone in the world.

When Sierra clapped, Oliver clapped. When Sierra booed, Oliver booed.

One of Oliver's favorite songs these days is "Take Me Out to the Ballgame," and I don't think I'm imagining it that when he gets to the part that goes, "I don't care if I ever get back," he gets a moony look on his face, remembering his day at the ballpark and how Sierra taught him everything he wanted to know about the game.

Taking Along the Kids

Struggling through the security check-in line at the airport in Florida, I thought, *This is why people avoid traveling with children.* Oliver had a lot of energy and what was required to keep him in the long line was nonstop redirection and physical restraint.

"I need to go over there!' Oliver repeatedly insisted, pointing off into an empty area near the windows. I was momentarily reminded of Tina Fey's daughter's catchphrase, which made it onto the show *30 Rock*: "I want to go to there."

Controlling him, plus all our bags, had aged me years in just a few minutes. Finally at the front of the line, I sensed relief. He could run around at the gate. I could get a coffee. Everything would be great.

But when we got to the front of the line, we realized Neal did not have his ID. It was somewhere in Florida, but not in any of our pockets or bags. "I'm going to have to stay in Florida!" he wailed, while we rifled through a million bags under the watchful eye of the security guard and Oliver repeated his inconvenient plea to be elsewhere.

Long story short: you can get on an airplane without government-issued ID. (Whether this is possible if you don't have a screaming toddler in tow and are holding up the line is not known.)

When I was doing last-minute planning for our D.C. trip to President Obama's inauguration, I saw on a few Web sites that a great many people were bailing on the trip because it seemed too hard to bring the kids.[19]

It was going to be cold and crowded. There would be no heated areas, no changing tables. The ticketed areas banned strollers and food. Some commenters insisted it was "child abuse" to even consider taking a toddler. One person told me he was going to leave his infant daughter with her grandparents but tell her later she had been there—maybe even that "Obama had brought her up onstage, Courtney-Cox-at-a-Springsteen-concert-style." An NPR headline cautioned, "Think Twice Before Bringing Kids to Inaugural."

I wondered if we should cancel the trip.

But my best friend and her kids were expecting us, and we couldn't exchange the train tickets. Besides, Neal and I wanted Oliver to be a witness to history, even if he wouldn't necessarily remember it. "I just wanted to be here" was the title of the CNN home page the morning of the inauguration, and that's exactly how I felt.

So we packed a bunch of warm clothes, decided we'd try to watch from the back of the Mall, near the Lincoln Memorial, where it wouldn't be so crowded, and bring a ton of Goldfish crackers.

We were cold, yes, in spite of our many layers. I had to hand-feed Oliver a sandwich because he couldn't concentrate on eating. I had to walk him around for the hour leading up to the oath while he complained about the wind. "It is magical here," I quasi-ironically texted my coworkers while standing inside a Port-a-Potty while Oliver repeatedly opened and closed the lock for entertainment.

And there were definite hassles. When we got off the train in D.C., we faced a two-hundred-person–long taxi line with no cabs in sight (who knew there would be a black-tie party at the train station the very night we were arriving?). If we'd been alone, Neal and I could have just walked across town in the cold and dark without worrying about Oliver freezing or about what we would do with the car seat.

As I bounced Oliver while he fussed, I said, "Okay, so maybe this whole trip seems like a terrible idea. But maybe it won't look that way later. We'll wait to judge this. We won't judge it now. We'll judge it on Thursday." And sure enough, by Thursday the cold couple of hours on the taxi line were practically forgotten. (It helped that right when I was losing hope of us ever getting away from that train station, Oliver's well-chosen godmother Tara drove into the swarm of tuxedoed humanity and rescued us.)

But once we were there at the event itself, actually on the Mall watching Obama take the oath and deliver his Inaugural Address, every annoyance seemed utterly insignificant. I've never experienced anything like being in a crowd of millions of silent, rapt people, nor will I probably ever again. I looked down at my son, sitting on my lap under a sleeping bag, staring at the Jumbotron, hypnotized by Obama's face and voice, and the speech hit home in a way it might not have had I been unencumbered. Obama said

For as much as government can do and must do, it is ulti-mately the faith and determination of the American people upon which this nation relies. It is the kindness to take in a stranger when the levees break, the selflessness of workers

who would rather cut their hours than see a friend lose their job, which sees us through our darkest hours. It is the fire-fighter's courage to storm a stairway filled with smoke, but also a parent's willingness to nurture a child, that finally de-cides our fate.

Showing up toddler in tow was a product of faith and de-termination. I looked around us at our fellow Americans on the Mall and I just *liked* them. All of them. There were two people in wheelchairs in front of us, a little girl and her mother to our side. There were people from every state and from abroad. No one had an easy time getting there, but once in the crowd together, we became one mass of joy. When Obama was officially proclaimed president, it was like a cork coming out of a bottle, everyone crying and laughing and hugging each other. An old white woman and an old black man next to us linked arms and spun each other in a circle. I've never felt prouder to be an American or more hopeful for our future.

One woman on the news said she had been there for the 1963 March on Washington, but that this was different, be-cause we had all gathered not to protest, but to give thanks. There were volunteer high-fivers lining the pathways when we entered the Mall, and everyone on the grounds smiled at one another. When Oliver said, "Barack Obama!" the people stand-ing around us rushed to give him fist bumps.

It's funny what my son remembers of that day on the Mall. He tells people that it was cold, that the reflecting pool was made of ice, that he saw "Barack Obama's car" (the motorcade on the Jumbotron made a big impression). He fondly remembers the Port-a-Potties. He wishes he could have given Obama cookies like he did the neighborhood firefighters at Christmas. And he recalls "a lot of people standing." When he gets older and realizes why they were standing, and laughing, and crying all around us, I hope he will be as grateful as I am that he was there.

Taking the kids along wherever you go isn't easier or harder necessarily; it's just different. They say cats are very territorial but that you can teach them to go for walks like dogs if they can equate you with their territory. Properly trained, as long as the cat is on your shoulder, you can be at your house or at a baseball game, and the cat is just as secure.

Young kids are like this. If they're in your arms, they don't much mind if they're on your couch at home or out on the town (although I've found those little headphones they sell at gun stores are good for fireworks or concerts). But it sure does matter to you. It gets superboring sitting on the couch all the time. And you can start resenting your kid. But it's not your kid that's keeping you from doing things. It's your obligation to a sense of the kind of parent you're supposed to be. The truth is, your kid just wants to be around you. He doesn't care if he's eating organic puffs or engaged in the most exclusive "Mommy and Me" classes money can buy.

But why bother? You'll hear. *Why bring them when they won't remember it?* Well, the latest research shows that even if they don't remember what they saw or did, they do remember how it made them feel. Psychotherapist Heather Turgeon writes

> *Without a mature hippocampus, babies and toddlers are mainly creatures of short-term memory. But the unconscious*

memories that they form right from the start may be the most important ones. These are the emotional patterns that we learn—that we are safe, that when mom picks us up we feel happy, or that when we knock over a tower of blocks and turn to look at dad, he will be smiling back at us. This is why many people say that the first few years of life are the most important—because way in the back of our brains is where we learn (unconsciously) that the world is a good place.[20]

We've taken Oliver to Greece, an outdoor Beastie Boys concert (again, headphones) in Brooklyn, to baseball spring training in Florida, on planes and trains and to every museum and neighborhood in New York City.

No, he won't remember Nick Evans's grand slam at that game in Port Saint Lucie. He won't remember the Acropolis. He won't remember the Beastie Boys coming backstage and going right up to him as he played with a bucket of ice. But he will remember, I think, the feeling of security and novelty that comes with being carried around in new places all the time, of meeting nice new people every day, of us soothing him to sleep on a trans-Atlantic trip.

And for whatever reason, some things seem to stick with him month after month. He remembers hot dogs at the ballpark in Florida. He remembers the firehouse headquarters in Cambridge, where we stopped for a tour and a T-shirt. He remembers sitting upstairs at my parents' house in the country watching his grandfather's Fourth of July fireworks alongside his cousins and friends, all of them staring out into the night, sipping chocolate milk.

It's always fun to see what kids pick up on. Our musician

friends had their son at an outdoor gig of theirs and thought seeing Mommy and Daddy onstage would make a big impression. What did their son remember? "Boats!" (You could see, off in the distance, some boats on a river.)

Daily Show correspondent Samantha Bee says of her kids, "We took them to the circus a while ago and they loved it. Well, Piper loved it because we allowed her to have a snow cone and Fletcher was just mesmerized. He loved the whole experience. You didn't hear a peep out of him the whole time. He was really entranced and Piper was just totally preoccupied by staring down at her snow cone. While people were flying overhead on the trapeze, we were like, 'Look up! Look up!' and she was like, 'I don't think you understand what is going on. I have a snow cone.'"[21]

I heard about one couple, forced to return early from a romantic two-week European vacation because their kid back home got sick, saying with a disgruntled sigh: "Well, I guess we'll just have to put our lives on hold for eighteen years."

As if the kid is not part of their lives!

A doctor I know told me that he took his young son and wife along to a medical conference and that on that trip his son had his first ice cream soda. "And the sight of him eating that ice cream, it dripping down his face while he smiled, is something I'll never forget," he said. "It's one of my happiest memories."

Yes, the doctor had to hang out in the hotel room after his son went to sleep. This meant missing some of the wild doctor parties, but he and his wife got room service and watched TV and had a perfectly lovely time while their happy, sun-kissed little boy slept nearby.

If you let go of some idea of what your life is supposed to be like, of what your life used to be, you can really get into this new life. It's not so hard to feed and clothe and shelter another human being for eighteen years, because love makes you want to do all those things and inspires you to find ways to manage it.

Battling the Jinx

Apparently, I just wrote a book about parenting. But I'm still no expert. Not only do I not have a degree in parenting. Not only is my child under the age of three. Not only have I had meltdowns and snapped and earned only a passing grade on the work-home balance test. But what's more, the second I think I've figured out something for sure, I'm proved totally, embarrassingly wrong.

That's right: I am a firm believer in the jinx.

To illustrate: Recently, Oliver's friend Aims was over and they were playing together so sweetly. Beaming with pride, Aims's father and I started to enthusiastically talk trash about other kids and other parents. We patted ourselves on the back for our superior skills. We spoke condescendingly about how easy it is, really, to make kids behave, to set boundaries, to create decent, darling little people like our sons.

Then—of course!—from the next room we heard screams. When we ran in, we saw our lovely little boys wrestling over a Thomas train—and not just wrestling, but also clawing, kicking, grabbing, and shrieking. They were practically frothing at the mouth. Since we didn't have a garden hose available to spray them with, we simply separated them by force, took away their trains, put them in time-out in separate rooms, and looked sheepishly at each other for the whole two minutes.

For the rest of the afternoon, even as our boys regained their composure and charmingly shared their toys, we remained humble. When we mentioned other kids and parents whom we'd usually relish trading horror stories about, we stayed mum on their faults. Our sons are wonderful, but we had been reminded by the Thomas smackdown that they are still children, and even the loveliest children are not yet fully civilized (and even when, or if, fully civilized, they will still have bad days).

Aims's father and his wife, and Neal and I, may be doing reasonably okay with our kids so far, but that doesn't mean anything, really. All we can do is love them and try not to get distracted by silly things that don't matter, like what new parenting philosophy to adopt or which stroller to buy. All we really have to do is remember that our sole job as parents is to raise our children up into decent human beings who are kind and responsible. Luckily, there are as many ways to accomplish that goal as there are parents in the world.

After my son went to sleep last night, I left my husband watching the Mets game and went to a friend's birthday party at a bar in the city. I was talking to the birthday girl (turning thirty for the ninth time) when two of her friends came over to say hi.

"What's new?" she asked them.

"We're engaged and having a baby!" the man cheered.

His fiancée smiled and pulled her cardigan aside to reveal a distinctly pregnant belly. "Five months along," she said pointing to it, looking astonished herself. "We're pretty excited about it," she said, trying to sound nonchalant and failing utterly. There were hugs all around.

This young couple looked kind of dazed and scared and giddy and radiant. And I thought, who knows what their plans are for breastfeeding, for work-home balance, for gear or child-care, or TV before two. They're having a *baby*. That baby is pure potential, and so are his giggly, freaked-out parents-to-be. You could just tell from looking at them: they were going to love that child and do their very best by him. Mistakes would be made, sure; fights would be had. And yet, the three of them, I sensed, would be just fine.

Endnotes

PART ONE

1. "Number, Timing, and Duration of Marriages and Divorces: 1996," Census Bureau Household Economic Studies, February 2002.
2. I recommend the breathtakingly depressing ABC show *Family* (1976–1980).
3. "Questions and Answers about Generation X/Generation Y," Sloan Work & Family Research Network Fact Sheet, Boston: Boston College, November 2008.
4. Thom Patterson, "Welcome to the 'Weisure' Lifestyle," CNN.com, May 11, 2009.
5. Meghan Pleticha, "3 Most Common Mistakes: Decorating Your Nursery," Babble.com, December 12, 2008.
6. "Family Begs Strangers for a Million Dollars," Gawker.com, December 6, 2007.
7. Susan Gregory Thomas, "Trouble at Home," Babble.com, December 22, 2008.
8. "Understanding Generational Differences in Home Remodeling Behavior," a study published by the Joint Center for Housing Studies at Harvard University (JCHS), Fall 2005, confirmed Gen X's obsession with details. (Referenced in "Trouble at Home," above.)
9. Comment by "Beth" on "The Pre-Baby Cloud of Deception: Is It Better to Be in the Dark About How Hard Parenting Really Is?" Jessica Ashley, Strollerderby.com, August 14, 2007.
10. Gwynne Watkins, "I'm Pregnant—Tell Me Something Good!" Strollerderby.com, August 16, 2007.
11. Susan Maushart, *The Mask of Motherhood: How Becoming a Mother Changes Our Lives and Why We Never Talk About It*, New York City: New Press, 1999, p. xx.

12. "Women Outnumber Men Among College Graduates," *Morning Edition*, NPR, May 17, 2005.

13. Sam Roberts, "Shift Emerges in Wage Gap Between the Sexes," *New York Times*, August 3, 2007.

14. "Covered employers must grant an eligible employee up to a total of 12 workweeks of unpaid leave during any 12-month period for one or more of the following reasons: for the birth and care of the newborn child of the employee." Family and Medical Leave Act, U.S. Department of Labor, 1993.

15. "Statutory Maternity Leave is for 52 weeks. You may be entitled to receive Statutory Maternity Pay for up to 39 weeks of the leave." http://www.direct.gov.uk/

16. Dr. Laura Schlessinger, *In Praise of Stay-at-Home Moms*, New York City: Harper, 2009.

17. Meg Wolitzer, "Baby vs. Career," Babble.com, May 19, 2008.

18. Sylvia Ann Hewlett, "Off-Ramps and On-Ramps," Huffington Post, June 4, 2007.

19. Lisa Belkin, "The Opt-Out Revolution," *New York Times*, October 26, 2003.

20. Amy Reiter, "Interview: Julianne Moore," Babble.com, March 23, 2009.

21. Adapted from Ada Calhoun, "What I Wouldn't Do for My Cat," Salon.com, February 8, 2008.

22. Ellen Gamerman, "Bad Parents and Proud of It: Moms and a Dad Confess," *Wall Street Journal*, April 13, 2009.

23. Rebecca Traister, "The Worst Parents in the World," Salon.com, May 6, 2009.

24. Katie Allison Granju, "Navel-Gazing Their Way Through Parenthood," Salon.com, October 21, 2003.

25. Kara Jesella, "Naughty Mommies," *The American Prospect*, April 3, 2009.

26. Bernard Carl Rosen, *Masks and Mirrors: Generation X and the Chameleon Personality*, Westport, Conn.: Praeger Publishers, 2001, p. 57.

27. L.J. Williamson, "TV or Not TV," Babble.com, March 23, 2008.

28. Liza Featherstone, "Be Afraid, Be Very Afraid," Babble.com, April 6, 2009.

29. Ada Calhoun, "5-Minute Time Out: *Follow That Bird*," Babble.com, March 29, 2009.

30. Babble.com poll archives.

31. Adapted from Ada Calhoun, "Political Partners," Nerve.com, February 4, 2008.

32. Patrick Healy, "For Clintons, Delicate Dance of Married and Public Lives," *New York Times*, May 23, 2006.

33. Anna Kuchment, "Father Time," *Newsweek*, October 11, 2007.

34. Jerry Adler, "Building a Better Dad," *Newsweek*, June 17, 1996.

35. Katha Pollitt, *Learning to Drive: And Other Life Stories*, New York City: Random House, 2007.

36. Excerpts from our conversation were published as "5-Minute Time Out: Katha Pollitt," Ada Calhoun, Babble.com, November 27, 2007.

37. John Mordechai Gottman, *What Predicts Divorce?: The Relationship Between Marital Processes and Marital Outcomes*, Mahwah, N.J.: Lawrence Erlbaum Associates, 1994, p. 110.

38. Adapted from Ada Calhoun, "Editor's Note: The Parental Clock," Babble .com, May 24, 2007.

39. Dr. Tara Bishop, M.D., "Dr. Mom," Babble.com, May 21, 2007.

40. Helaine Olen, "5-Minute Time Out: Pamela Stone," Babble.com, May 24, 2007.

41. A good essay on this topic is Jeanne Sager's "Dads Don't Babysit," Babble .com, May 6, 2009.

42. Barbara Ehrenreich, *The Hearts of Men: American Dreams and the Flight from Commitment*, New York City: Anchor Books, 1983.

43. Susan Gregory Thomas, "Today's Tykes: Secure Kids or Rudest in History?" MSNBC.com, May 6, 2009.

44. Dr. Perri Klass, "Making Room for Miss Manners Is a Parenting Basic," *New York Times*, January 12, 2009.

45. Melissa Rayworth, "The Sleepless Generation," Babble.com, May 12, 2008.

46. M. Suzanne Zeedyk, "One Ride Forward, Two Steps Back," *New York Times* op-ed, March 1, 2009.

47. http://www.cdc.gov/SafeChild/

48. Joanne Kaufman, "When Grandma Can't Be Bothered," *New York Times*, March 4, 2009.

49. Ann Zimmerman, "Grandma or Grandpa by Any Other Name Is Just as Old," *Wall Street Journal*, January 23, 2009.

50. Ann Hulbert, *Raising America: Experts, Parents, and a Century of Advice About Children*, New York City: Knopf, 2003.

51. Selma H. Fraiberg, *The Magic Years: Understanding and Handling the Problems of Early Childhood*, New York City: Scribner, 1996.

52. Kara Jesella, "The New Eugenics," Babble.com, May 22, 2009.

PART TWO

1. Environmental Working Group, "Shopper's Guide to Pesticides," Foodnews.org, 2009.

2. Brett Berk, "In Praise of Junk," Babble.com, March 9, 2009.

3. Jennifer Block, "The Backlash to Breast is Best," Babble.com, April 21, 2009.

4. Madeline Holler, "Parenting Trends," Babble.com, July 8, 2008.

PART THREE

1. Adapted from Ada Calhoun, "Editor's Note: You'll Be a Man, My Son," Babble.com, March 6, 2007.

2. Hanna Otero, "Resentment," Babble.com, January 22, 2009.

3. Parts of our conversation were published as "5-Minute Time Out: Penelope Leach," Babble.com, May 7, 2009.

4. Deborah Kotz, "A Risky Rise in C-Sections," *U.S. News & World Report*, March 28, 2008.

5. Tova Mirvis, "In Praise of the C-Section," Babble.com, March 31, 2009.

6. Kathryn J. Alexander, "Insufferable," Babble.com, February 17, 2007.

7. "The rate of victimization decreased from 12.2 per 1,000 children in 2003 to 10.6 per 1,000 children in 2007," U.S. Department of Health and Human Services (HHS), Figure 3-1: Child Disposition and Victimization Rates, 2003–2007.

8. Christopher Noxon, "Parents Unite! Ban Birthday Party Blowouts," Reuters, May 5, 2008.

9. Tina Kelley, "Cake, but No Presents, Please," *New York Times*, July 27, 2007.

10. Amy S. F. Lutz, "Presents, Please," Babble.com, October 29, 2007.

11. Asra Q. Nomani, "Birthdays Gone Wild!" Babble.com, April 25, 2007.

12. Kim Brooks, "The Sickest Baby on the Block," Babble.com, March 12, 2009.

13. Richard Weissbourd, *The Parents We Mean to Be: How Well-Intentioned Adults Undermine Children's Moral and Emotional Development*, Boston: Houghton Mifflin Harcourt, 2009.

14. Rebecca Walker, *Baby Love: Choosing Motherhood After a Lifetime of Ambivalence*, New York City: Riverhead Books, 2007.

15. Gwynne Watkins, "5-Minute Time Out: Dr. Paul Offit, M.D.," Babble.com, March 2, 2009.

16. "American Academy of Pediatrics: Circumcision Policy Statement," *Pediatrics* vol. 103, no. 3 (March 1999), pp. 686–693. Statement of reaffirmation published September 1, 2005.

17. Cole Gamble, "A Guy's Take on Why You Shouldn't Circumcise (and Why You Should)," Strollerderby.com, October 13, 2008.

ENDNOTES

18. Miriam Axel-Lute, "Toddlers in Love," Babble.com, February 12, 2009.
19. Adapted from Ada Calhoun, "Editor's Note: On Taking the Kids," Babble.com, January 27, 2009.
20. Heather Turgeon, "Memento," Babble.com, January 12, 2009.
21. Christina Couch, "Interview: Samantha Bee," Babble.com, February 9, 2009.

Acknowledgments

Thank you: Lisa Crystal Carver; Dr. Elihu Sussman, Logan Hill, Erica Pirchio, Hannah Harvey Alderson, Rhoades Alderson, Kara Jesella, Jessica Valenti, Lili Taylor, Kenny Mellman, Brendan Kennedy, and everyone at Waywaw; everyone at Williamsburg Neighborhood Nursery School; Ondine Galsworth, Kathy Lilleskov, Michael Martin, David Kelly, Dr. Eric Hess, Gary Simmons, Asia Wong, Nancy Cardozo, and Mark Jacobson, everyone on The Pressure softball team, especially Kathleen Hanna, Juliana Luecking, and Adam Horovitz; everyone at Babble.com, especially Gwynne Watkins, April Peveteaux, and our writers; everyone in Southside Williamsburg, especially Guy, Rebecca, Nikita, Noah, Johanna, Jim, Yvette, Shorty, Engine Company 221, Zaida, and Gloria; all the wonderful kids in our life and our sons', including Aims, Ella, Mars, Harper, Sam, Maeve, Curtis, Liberty, Lidia Jean, Julia, Xander, and Jacob; my better-than-fine parents, Peter Schjeldahl and Brooke Alderson; my father-in-law, Lanny Medlin; my smart and supportive editor, Patrick Price, plus Tricia Boczkowski and everyone else at Gallery Books; Peter Steinberg, the loveliest agent in the history of agent-kind; my best friend, Tara McKelvey; my husband, the incredible artist known as Neal Medlyn; and my son, Oliver Gary, and stepson, Andrew Blake, the two best boys in the whole world.